Packet Analysis with Wireshark

Leverage the power of Wireshark to troubleshoot your
networking issues by using effective packet analysis
techniques and performing an improved protocol analysis

Anish Nath

[PACKT] **open source** ✳
PUBLISHING   community experience distilled

BIRMINGHAM - MUMBAI

Packet Analysis with Wireshark

First published: November 2015

Production reference: 1261115

Published by Packt Publishing Ltd.
Livery Place
35 Livery Street
Birmingham B3 2PB, UK.

ISBN 978-1-78588-781-9

www.packtpub.com

Credits

Author
Anish Nath

Reviewers
Michael Downey

Robert Juric

Mikael Kanstrup

Acquisition Editor
Indrajit Das

Content Development Editor
Rohit Singh

Technical Editor
Mrunmayee Patil

Copy Editor
Stephen Copestake

Project Coordinator
Mary Alex

Proofreader
Safis Editing

Indexer
Monica Ajmera Mehta

Production Coordinator
Nilesh Mohite

Cover Work
Nilesh Mohite

About the Author

Anish Nath is a software engineer who has more than 10 years of experience. He works at CISCO, and at CISCO, he started using Wireshark for the first time. He is thankful to CISCO. He doesn't speak much, but likes to explore new things that he has not tried or not thought of. He also tries his best to be successful at this. Though he fails a lot of time, this gives him more experience, and when success comes, he thanks all of his efforts that had failed him initially.

You can reach him at `https://in.linkedin.com/in/anishnath`, and his Twitter handle is `@anish2good`.

I would like to thank my friends, Arnab Biswas, Arun John, Ganesh Choudhari, Mayank Johari, Pradeep Sivakumar, Prakash John, Deepak Kukrety, and Veeksha Vasant for supporting me in this venture. I've definitely learned a lot from their experience.

I would also like to thank, Alice Chen, Tin Nguyen, Sunil Menon, Saad Abderrazzaq, Ori Lior, Mahin Khani, Donn Coe, Rob Andrews, and Lon Barrett, for their support and belief in me all this time and also for providing me assistance when I needed it.

Special thanks to the Wireshark community and its developers for writing an awesome tool like this.

Thanks to all my reviewers who made an effort so that this book took the correct shape.

My apologies if I've missed anyone.

Thanks to Packt Publishing and the entire team, especially Indrajit Das and Rohit Singh for making this happen.

About the Reviewers

Michael Downey is a security analyst with a passion for *nix operating systems and network security monitoring. He is also the cofounder of the Evansville Linux User Group in Indiana, and a contributing member of OpenNSM (`http://www.open-nsm.net/`). In his free time, he enjoys security research and an occasional game of disc golf.

Robert Juric, while working as a network engineer, has supported government agencies, large corporations, and service providers. From his experience, he learned the value of packet analysis and has come to enjoy the details that it provides.

When not at work, Robert enjoys spending time outdoors with his wife and young son. He occasionally writes articles for his website, `robertjuric.com`, or can be found on Twitter at `@robertj180`.

Mikael Kanstrup is a software engineer with a passion for adventure and thrills in life. In his spare time, he spends his time kitesurfing, riding motocross, or just going outdoors with his family and two kids. Mikael has a BSc degree in computer science and years of experience in embedded software development and computer networking. For the past decade, he has been working as a professional software developer in the mobile phone industry.

www.PacktPub.com

Support files, eBooks, discount offers, and more

For support files and downloads related to your book, please visit www.PacktPub.com.

Did you know that Packt offers eBook versions of every book published, with PDF and ePub files available? You can upgrade to the eBook version at www.PacktPub.com and as a print book customer, you are entitled to a discount on the eBook copy. Get in touch with us at service@packtpub.com for more details.

At www.PacktPub.com, you can also read a collection of free technical articles, sign up for a range of free newsletters and receive exclusive discounts and offers on Packt books and eBooks.

https://www2.packtpub.com/books/subscription/packtlib

Do you need instant solutions to your IT questions? PacktLib is Packt's online digital book library. Here, you can search, access, and read Packt's entire library of books.

Why subscribe?

- Fully searchable across every book published by Packt
- Copy and paste, print, and bookmark content
- On demand and accessible via a web browser

Free access for Packt account holders

If you have an account with Packt at www.PacktPub.com, you can use this to access PacktLib today and view 9 entirely free books. Simply use your login credentials for immediate access.

I would like to dedicate this book to my 5-year old son, Arjun Nath; grandfather, Sri Rajeshwar Prasad; wife, Manisha Prasad; mother, Indu Sinha; and all my family members (my father, Anil Kumar Sinha; chote papa, Sunil Kumar Sinha; choti mummy, Poonam Sinha; and friends). Without them, this would not have been possible.

Table of Contents

Preface

The purpose of this book is to identify, learn about, and solve issues related to protocol, network, and security, and see how Wireshark helps to analyze these patterns by allowing its features to troubleshoot effectively. This book has lab exercises and contains packet capture files for offline viewing and analyses. Most of the examples contain production-like scenarios and their solutions and steps to reproduce these solutions.

This book also contains effective capturing methods that can be used directly in production without installing Wireshark.

Wireshark is an awesome tool for troubleshooting and learning, and within the scope of this book, we have taken the best use cases for different types of audiences, such as network administrators, security auditors, protocol learners, and troubleshooters.

What this book covers

Chapter 1, Packet Analyzers, covers the definition of packet analyzers and their use cases, network interfaces naming conventions, pcap/pcanpng file extensions, and types of network analyzer tools.

Chapter 2, Capturing Packets, covers how to capture packets using Wireshark, tcpdump, and snoop; how to use Wireshark display filters; and how to use Wireshark's cool features such as Decode-As and protocol preferences. Also, we will cover the TCP stream, exporting images, generating a firewall ACL rule, autocapture setup, and the name resolution feature.

Chapter 3, Analyzing the TCP Network, covers the TCP state machine, TCP connection establishment and closing sequence, practical troubleshooting labs such as (CLOSE_WAIT, TIME_WAIT), how to identify and fix latency issues, and Wireshark TCP sequence analysis flag (zero window, dup-ok, TCP retransmission, and window update) features.

Chapter 4, *Analyzing SSL/TLS*, covers the TLS/SSL two-way mutual authentication process with Wireshark, SSL/TLS decryption with Wireshark, and the identification of handshake failure with Wireshark.

Chapter 5, *Analyzing Application Layer Protocols*, covers how to analyze a protocol using the Wireshark display filter, how these protocols work, how to simulate these packets, capture, and display them using tcpdump/Wireshark.

Chapter 6, *WLAN Capturing*, covers WLAN capture setup and monitor mode, capturing with tcpdump, 802.11 display filters, Layer-2 datagram frames types, Wireshark display filters, and other Wi-Fi Sniffing products available.

Chapter 7, *Security Analysis*, covers the security aspect with Wireshark and discusses uses cases such as the Heartbleed bug, SYN flood/mitigation, ICMP flood/ mitigation, MITM, BitTorrent, and host scanning.

What you need for this book

The topics covered in this book require a basic understanding of TCP/IP. The examples used in this book are independent of an operating system. All the examples are executed in a MAC and Linux OS. Windows users can install Cygwin to use a Linux command-line utility. The following executables are used in this book:

- Wireshark
- tcpdump
- snoop
- dig
- nslookup
- java
- wget
- dhclient
- nmap

Who this book is for

This book provides background information to help readers understand the topics that are discussed. The intended audience for this book includes the following:

- Network/system administrators
- Security consultants and IT officers
- Architects/protocol developers
- White Hat hackers

Conventions

In this book, you will find a number of text styles that distinguish between different kinds of information. Here are some examples of these styles and an explanation of their meaning.

Code words in text, database table names, folder names, filenames, file extensions, pathnames, dummy URLs, user input, and Twitter handles are shown as follows: "Start Wireshark by clicking on the Wireshark icon or type `Wireshark` in the command line."

Any command-line input or output is written as follows:

```
[bash ~]# cat /proc/sys/net/ipv4/tcp_fin_timeout 60
```

New terms and **important words** are shown in bold. Words that you see on the screen, for example, in menus or dialog boxes, appear in the text like this: "Click on **Interface List**; Wireshark will show a list of available network interfaces in the system."

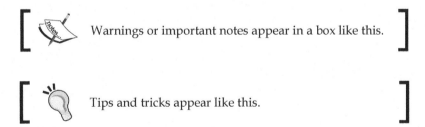

Warnings or important notes appear in a box like this.

Tips and tricks appear like this.

Reader feedback

Feedback from our readers is always welcome. Let us know what you think about this book—what you liked or disliked. Reader feedback is important for us as it helps us develop titles that you will really get the most out of.

To send us general feedback, simply e-mail feedback@packtpub.com, and mention the book's title in the subject of your message.

If there is a topic that you have expertise in and you are interested in either writing or contributing to a book, see our author guide at www.packtpub.com/authors.

Customer support

Now that you are the proud owner of a Packt book, we have a number of things to help you to get the most from your purchase.

Downloading the example code

You can download the example code files from your account at http://www.packtpub.com for all the Packt Publishing books you have purchased. If you purchased this book elsewhere, you can visit http://www.packtpub.com/support and register to have the files e-mailed directly to you.

Errata

Although we have taken every care to ensure the accuracy of our content, mistakes do happen. If you find a mistake in one of our books—maybe a mistake in the text or the code—we would be grateful if you could report this to us. By doing so, you can save other readers from frustration and help us improve subsequent versions of this book. If you find any errata, please report them by visiting http://www.packtpub.com/submit-errata, selecting your book, clicking on the **Errata Submission Form** link, and entering the details of your errata. Once your errata are verified, your submission will be accepted and the errata will be uploaded to our website or added to any list of existing errata under the Errata section of that title.

To view the previously submitted errata, go to `https://www.packtpub.com/books/content/support` and enter the name of the book in the search field. The required information will appear under the **Errata** section.

Piracy

Piracy of copyrighted material on the Internet is an ongoing problem across all media. At Packt, we take the protection of our copyright and licenses very seriously. If you come across any illegal copies of our works in any form on the Internet, please provide us with the location address or website name immediately so that we can pursue a remedy.

Please contact us at `copyright@packtpub.com` with a link to the suspected pirated material.

We appreciate your help in protecting our authors and our ability to bring you valuable content.

Questions

If you have a problem with any aspect of this book, you can contact us at `questions@packtpub.com`, and we will do our best to address the problem.

1
Packet Analyzers

A packet analyzer is also known as a packet sniffer or a network protocol analyzer. Packet analyzer has the ability to grab the raw packet from the wire, wireless, Bluetooth, VLAN, PPP, and other network types, without getting processed by the application. By doing so it brings the whole science and innovation to this field. In this chapter we will see a few use cases of the packet analyzer by covering the following topics:

- Uses for packet analyzers
- Introducing Wireshark
- Other packet analyzer tools
- Mobile packet capturing

Uses for packet analyzers

More practically, packet analyzers are employed in network security and to analyze raw traffic so as to detect scans and attacks, and for sniffing, network troubleshooting, and many more uses, as shown in the following image:

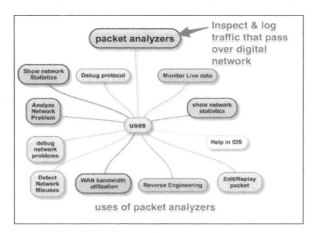

Packet analyzers can be used as follows:

- Network administrators can diagnose problems on a network
- Security architects can perform a security audit on a packet
- Protocol developers can diagnose/learn protocol-related issues
- White-hat hackers can find vulnerabilities in the application and fix them before black-hat hacker find them

The use is not limited to these bullet point, there are lots of new tools and innovations happening in this area. Find a use case and build your own packet analyzer; the best example is Wireshark.

Introducing Wireshark

Wireshark is perhaps one of the best open source packet analyzers available today. Wireshark is a powerful packet analyzer tool, with an easy-to-use, rich GUI and a command-line utility with very active community support: http://ask.wireshark.org.

Wireshark uses pcap (libpcap) to capture packets, which means it can capture packets in offline mode—to view the captured packets—and online mode (live traffic) to capture and display the traffic in the Wireshark GUI. Once open, the Wireshark GUI looks like this:

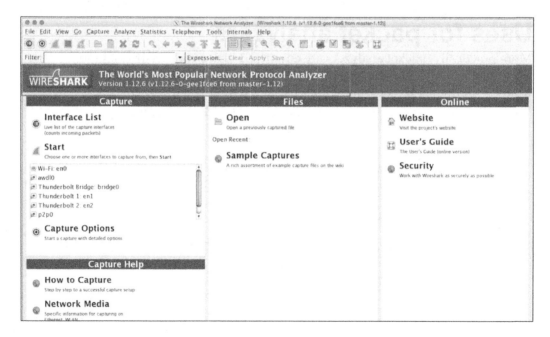

Wireshark features

We will see some of the important features that are available in Wireshark in the following figure:

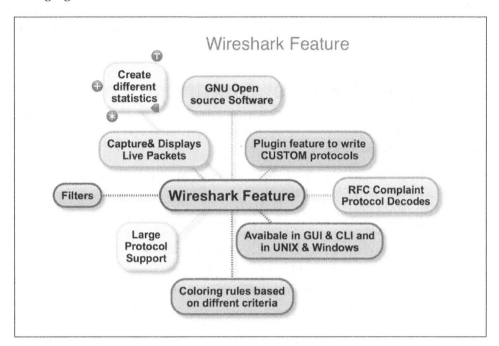

Wireshark has the following cool built-in features, few of them are listed as follows:

- Available in both UNIX and Windows
- Ability to capture live packets from various types of interface
- Filters packets with many criteria
- Ability to decode larger sets of protocols
- Can save and merge captured packets
- Can create various statistics
- User-friendly GUI and command-line interface
- Active community support (http://ask.wireshark.org)

Wireshark's dumpcap and tshark

The Wireshark installation provides some command-line tools such as dumpcap and tshark. Wireshark and tshark rely on dumpcap to capture traffic; more advanced functionality is performed by tshark. Also note that dumpcap can be run as its own standalone utility. tshark is a command-line version of Wireshark and can be used in the remote terminal.

The Wireshark packet capture process

The user must be aware of where Wireshark is installed and it should be obliged with your organization policy before start capturing on the **TAP** (**Test Access Point**) or **Switch Port Analyzer** (**SPAN**) port.

Usually developers install Wireshark on their personal laptop/desktop and capture packets, which goes in-out from the box.

Certain guidelines should be followed to perform this:

1. Make sure you're allowed to do what you're going to do; check your corporate policies before capturing a packet.
2. The operating system must support packet capturing:
    - Linux packet socket support is enabled in the kernel by default
    - Windows requires WinPCap to be installed
3. Choose the interface and enable the promiscuous mode on it. Promiscuous mode accepts all packets whether they are addressed to the interface or not.
4. If using a Wi-Fi interface, enable the monitor mode for WLAN capturing.
5. Start capturing and use Wireshark's different features like (filters/statistics/ IO/save) for further analysis

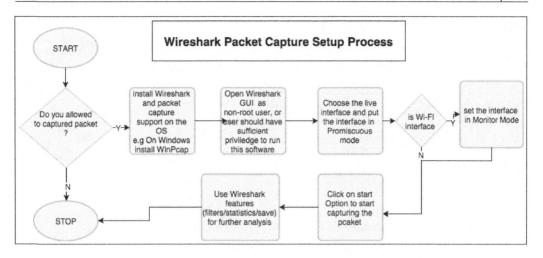

Other packet analyzer tools

Wireshark is a packet analysis tool to use features such as packet editing/replaying, performing MITM, ARPspoof, IDS, and HTTP proxy, and there are other packet analyzer tools available and can be used as well.

The following is a list (not limited) of notable packet analyzer tools on the market; many others are commercially available. The table lists tools and their features:

Tools	Packet editing	Packet replay	ARPspoof/ MITM	Password sniffing	Intrusion detection	HTTP debugger
WireEdit (https:// wireedit.com/)	Y	N	N	N	N	N
Scapy (http://www. secdev.org/)	Y	Y	Y	Y	N	Y
Ettercap (https:// ettercap.github.io/ ettercap/)	Y	N	Y	Y	N	N
Tcpreplay (http:// tcpreplay.synfin. net/)	N	Y	N	N	N	N
Bit-Twist (http:// bittwist. sourceforge.net/)	Y	N	N	N	N	N
Cain (http://www.oxid. it/cain.html)	N	N	Y	Y	N	N
Snort (https://www. snort.org/)	N	N	N	N	Y	N

Mobile packet capture

Wireshark is not available on mobile platforms such as Android, iOS, or Windows. In order to capture mobile traffic the following tools are suggested based on the platform:

Platform	Packet capture tool used	URL
Windows	Microsoft Network Analyzers	`http://www.microsoft.com/en-in/` `download/details.aspx?id=19484`
iOS	Paros	`http://sourceforge.net/projects/` `paros/`
Android	Shark for Root	`http://www.appbrain.com/app/shark-` `for-root/lv.n3o.shark`
	Kismet Android PCAP	`http://www.kismetwireless.net/` `android-pcap/`

Various other techniques are used to capture mobile traffic using Wireshark. One such technique is creating a Wi-Fi hotspot on the laptop, allowing the mobile phone to use this Wi-Fi, and sniffing traffic on your Wi-Fi interface using Wireshark.

Summary

In this chapter we learned what packet analyzers are and what their use cases are. After a quick introduction to Wireshark, we covered what goes on behind-the-scenes when Wireshark captures packets; Wireshark benefits and important features; the necessary prerequisites before capturing packets; and other packet analyzer tools for packet editing/sniffing/replaying and so on. We also provided a brief overview of mobile packet capturing.

The next chapter will be more specific to Wireshark and its tips and tricks. After that we will explore TCP troubleshooting, then plunge into SSL, and other application protocols such as DHCPv6, DHCP, DNS, and HTTP. We will also analyze Wi-Fi capturing and carry out some security analyses with the help of Wireshark and `tcpdump`.

2
Capturing Packets

In the previous chapter, we learned what packet analyzers are used for. In this chapter we will learn more about the Wireshark GUI features, and see how it helps in capturing and analyzing packets effectively, by covering the following topics:

- Capturing packets with Wireshark interface lists
- Capturing packets with Wireshark start options
- Capture options
- Wireshark filter examples
- Wireshark Packet List pane
- Wireshark Packet Details pane
- Wireshark features
- The tcpdump and snoop examples

Guide to capturing packets

Start Wireshark by clicking on the Wireshark icon or type `Wireshark` in the command line. When Wireshark starts it launches the following screen and provides the following ways to capture packets:

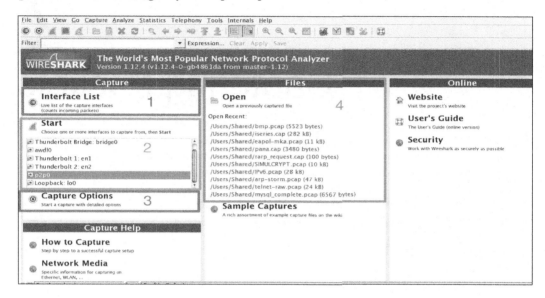

The following table explains the various options that we have on the Start screen:

Sr. no.	Wireshark capture options	What is this?
1	Interface List	Opens up a live list of capture interfaces, and counts the incoming/outgoing packets
2	Start	You can choose an interface from the list and start capturing packets
3	Capture Options	Provides various options for capturing and displaying packets
4	Open Recent	Wireshark displays recently used packets

We will cover each capturing option in detail one by one.

Capturing packets with Interface Lists

Click on **Interface List**; Wireshark will show a list of available network interfaces in the system and which one is active, by showing packets going in and out of the Interface, as shown in the following screenshot:

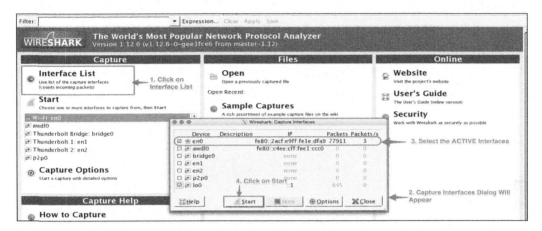

Choose the right (live) interfaces and click on the **Start** button to start capturing packets. If you want to capture packets on loopback (127.0.0.1), select the interface **lo0**.

Common interface names

The interface name tells you the network type; by looking at the name of the interface the user should understand what network the capture setup is associated with—for example, eth0 stands for Ethernet. A few of them are shown in the following diagram:

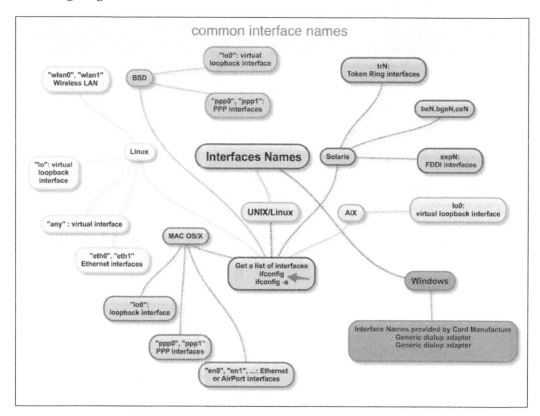

Capturing packets with Start options

In **Start** options, users can multiselect or select the interface displayed in the list and then click on Start. This doesn't give you the flexibility to see on which interface the packets are active. Users can configure the capture options by double clicking on the interface or by clicking on **Capture Options**:

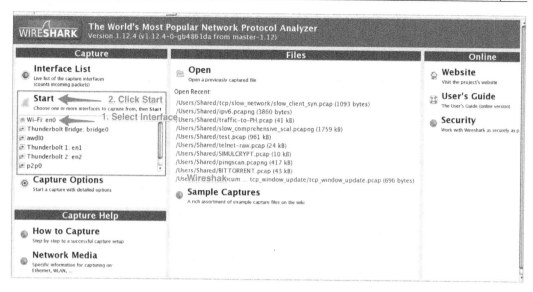

Capturing packets with Capture Options

Wireshark provides the flexibility to configure packets that need to be captured with various capture options. To begin, try these basic settings:

1. Choose the live interface, where packets are going in and out.

2. Click on **Capture Options**, Wireshark will open the **Capture Options** dialog box.

3. Enable the promiscuous mode, which will allow the network interface to receive all packets.

4. Check the snaplength size. This option will tell you the size of data for each frame that should be captured by Wireshark; this is useful when capturing the header frame or to keep the packet size small.

5. **Name Resolution** tries to resolve the numerical address (for example, the MAC address, the IP address, and port) to its corresponding name, under the category where the following options are defined:

   ° **Resolve MAC addresses**: This is used to convert the MAC address to a human-readable format; for example `28:cf:e9:1e:df:a9` will translate to `192.168.1.101`.

   ° **Resolve network-layer names** (IP name resolution): This is used to convert the IP address to its corresponding hostname (for example, `216.58.220.46` will translate to `google.com`).

- ° **Resolve transport-layer name** (TCP/UDP port name resolution): This is used to convert well-known ports to human-readable format (for example, `443` will translate to `https`).

6. Use the external network name resolver to perform a reverse DNS lookup for each unique IP address (for example `216.58.196.14` will translate to `ns4.google.com`) also referred to as reverse DNS lookup.

Users can also choose these options by selecting the Wireshark **View** menu and applying the following settings:

- **View | Name Resolution | Use External Network Name Resolver**
- **View | Name Resolution | Enable for MAC Layer**
- **View | Name Resolution | Enable for Transport Layer**
- **View | Name Resolution | Enable for Network Layer**

The drawbacks of name resolution are as follows:

- Once you have enabled these name resolution options, Wireshark will generate extra packets to resolve the name from the name server if the traffic is huge and there are high numbers of unique IP addresses. With these settings Wireshark will become very slow.
- Wireshark caches the resolved DNS name, so if the name server information changes, manual reload is required.

The capture filter options

Wireshark provides a range of capture filter options, use these options to decide which packets will save to the disk. These options are useful when capturing packets over a longer period of time. Wireshark uses the **Berkeley Packet Filter** (BPF) syntax for this purpose, for example `tcp src port 22`. This option also saves disk space. For example, to capture only TCP packets, follow the given steps:

1. Click on **Capture Options**. The dialog box will open as shown in the screenshot.
2. Select the *active* interface and set the promiscuous mode setting to enabled or disabled.

3. Click on **Capture Filter**. Once the dialog box appears, choose the
   TCP only filter and click on **OK**.

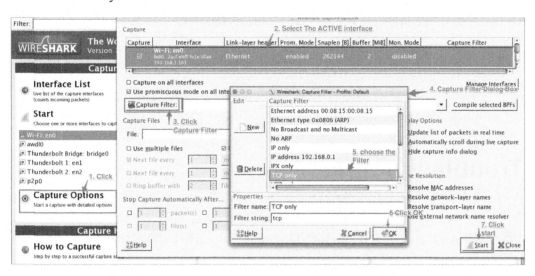

4. Click on the **Start** button to start capturing just the TCP packets.

Auto-capturing a file periodically

Users can fine-tune Wireshark to auto-capture files periodically. To do this, click on
Capture Options | Capture Files, as shown in the following screenshot:

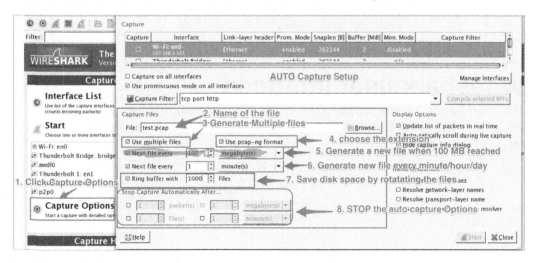

Wireshark will generate files such as `test_00001_20150623001728.pcap` and `test_00002_20150623001818.pcap`.

The formats of the multiple generated files are as follows:

- `test`: This is the filename
- `00001`: This is the file number
- `20150623001728`: This is the date/time stamp
- `pcap`: This is the file extension

Troubleshooting

If a packet doesn't appear in the Wireshark main window, perform the following actions:

- Check the right network interface; make sure there is live traffic
- Try turning off/on promiscuous mode

If no interface appears on which captures can be performed, do the following:

- Check if Wireshark has sufficient rights to use a network card to capture data
- Verify capture privileges from `http://wiki.wireshark.org/ CaptureSetup/CapturePrivileges`

 You can also use the Wireshark community at `https://ask. wireshark.org/` if queries aren't resolved.

Wireshark user interface

The Wireshark main window appears when Wireshark starts capturing a packet, or when a `.pcap` file is open for offline viewing. It looks similar to the following screenshot:

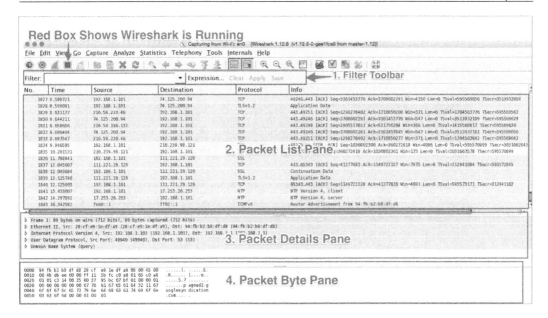

The Wireshark UI interface consists of different panes and provides various options to the user for customizing it. In this chapter, we will cover these panes in detail:

Item	What is it?
The red box	This shows that Wireshark is running and capturing a packet
1	This is the **Filter** toolbar, used for filtering packets based on the applied filter
2	This is the Packet List pane, which displays all captured packets
3	This is the Packet Details pane, which shows the selected packet in a verbose form
4	This is the Packet Byte pane, which shows the selected packet in a hex dump format

First, just observe pane **2** in the screen; the displayed packets appear with different colors. This is one of Wireshark's best features; it colors packets according to the set filter and helps you visualize the packet you are looking for.

To manage (view, edit, or create) a coloring rule, go to **View | Coloring Rules**. Wireshark will display the **Coloring Rules** dialog box, as shown in the screenshot:

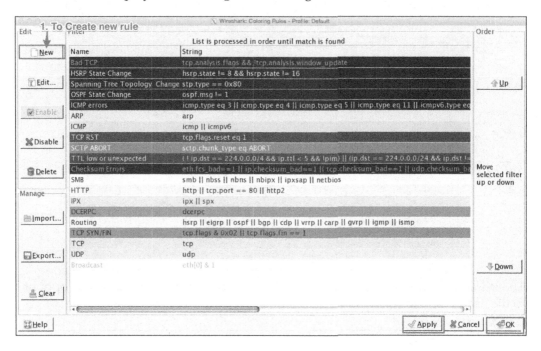

Users can create a new rule by clicking on the **New** button, choosing the filter name and filter string, and then applying a foreground and background color to it, to customize the packet with a specific color.

The Filter toolbar

The Wireshark display filter displays packets with its available coloring options. Wireshark display filters are used to change the view of a capture file by providing the full dissection of all packets, which helps analyzing a network tracefile efficiently. For example, if a user is interested in only HTTP packets, the user can set the display filter to `http`, as shown in the next screenshot.

The steps to apply display filters are as follows:

1. Open the `http_01.pcap` file.

2. Type the `http` protocol in the filter area and click on **Apply**.

Once the filter is applied, the Packet List pane will display only HTTP protocol-related packets:

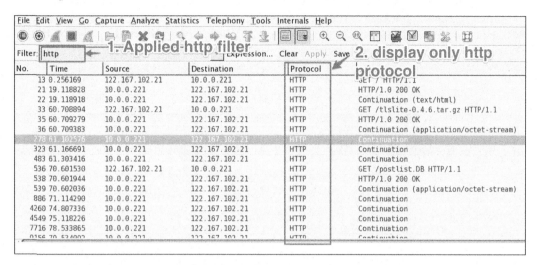

Wireshark display filter can be applied or prepared from the column displayed in the Packet List pane by selecting the column, then right-clicking and going to **Apply as Filter | Selected** (as shown in the following screenshot) to create the filter from the source IP address `122.167.102.21`:

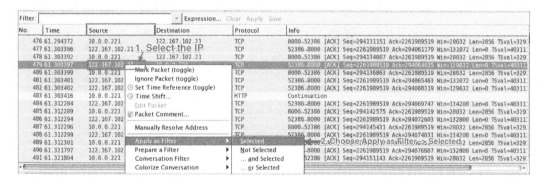

Wireshark provides the flexibility to apply filters from the Details pane; the steps remain the same.

Wireshark also provides the option to clear the filter. To do this click on **Clear** (available in the **Filter** toolbar) to display the entire captured packet.

Filtering techniques

Capturing and displaying packets properly will help you with packet captures. For example, to track a packet exchanged between two hosts: HOSTA (10.0.0.221) and HOSTB (122.167.99.148), open the SampleCapture01.pcap file and apply the filter ip.src == 10.0.0.221 as shown:

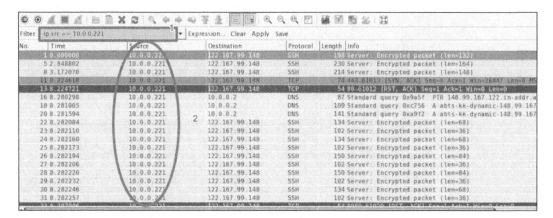

Let's see what the highlighted sections depict:

Item	Description
1	Apply filter ip.src == 10.0.0.221.
2	The Packet List pane displays the traffic from source to destination. The source shows the constant IP address 10.0.0.221. There is no evidence as to which packet is sent from host 122.167.99.148 to host 10.0.0.221.

Now modify the filter (ip.src == 10.0.0.221) && (ip.dst == 122.167.99.148) to (ip.src == 10.0.0.221) or (ip.dst == 122.167.99.148). This will give the result shown in the following screenshot:

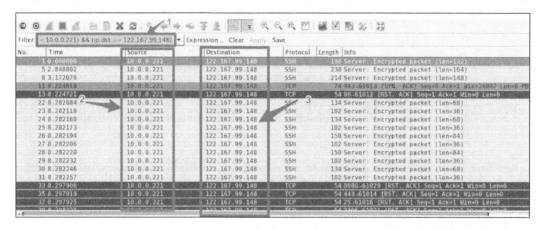

The highlighted sections in the preceding screenshot are explained as follows:

Item	Description
1	Applied filter (`ip.src == 10.0.0.221`) && (`ip.dst == 122.167.99.148`)
2	The source IP address (`10.0.0.221`) is not changed
3	The destination IP address (`122.167.99.148`) is not changed

Again the Packet List pane is not displaying the conversation between the two hosts.

Now modify the filter `ip.addr == 122.167.99.148`. The `ip.addr` field will match the IP header for both the source and destination address and display the conversation between the hosts. Remember to choose the destination IP address as shown:

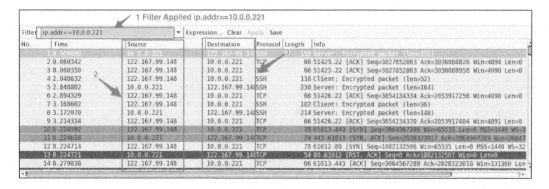

Let's see what the highlighted sections depict:

Item	Description
1	Applied filter `ip.addr == 122.167.99.148`
2	The source IP is not constant; it shows the conversation between the two hosts
3	The destination IP is not constant; it shows the conversation between the two hosts

The same conversation is captured by choosing the destination MAC address using the display filter `eth.addr == 06:73:7a:4c:2f:85`.

Filter examples

Some common filter examples are as follows:

Filter/capture name	Filter value
Packet on a given port	`tcp.port == 443`
Packet on the source port	`tcp.srcport=2222`
SYN packet on port 443	`(tcp.port == 443) && (tcp.flags == 0x0010)`
The HTTP protocol	`http`
Based on the HTTP `get` method	`http.request.method == "GET"`
Using `&&`, `tcp`, and `http`	`tcp && http`
Checking the `tcp` window size	`tcp.window_size <2000`
No Arp used for normal traffic	`!arp`
The MAC address filter	`eth.dst == 06:43:7b:4c:4f:85`
Filter out TCP ACK	`tcp.flags.ack==0`
Check only RST and ACK packets	`(tcp.flags.ack == 1) && (tcp.flags.reset == 1)`
Filter all SNMP	`Snmp`
HTTP or DNS or SSL	`http || dns	ssl`

There is no need to memorize the filter; there is an easy way to apply it. The display filter Autocomplete feature lists all dissectors after the first period "." that have been added to the display filter, as shown in the following screenshot:

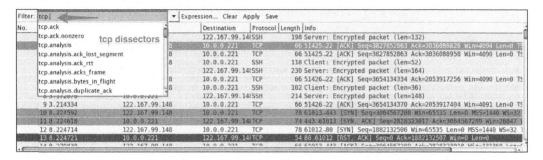

It's worth checking the following links for a complete display filter reference:

- Check out the TCP display filter reference: `https://www.wireshark.org/docs/dfref/t/tcp.html`
- Check out this alternative protocol display filter reference: `https://www.wireshark.org/docs/dfref/`

The Packet List pane

The Packet List pane displays packets from the `.pcap` (or accepted Wireshark extensions) file or from live capture, as shown:

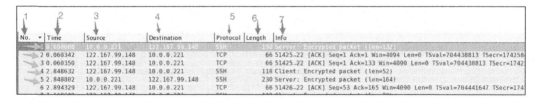

Let's discuss the fields shown:

Item	What is it?
➡	Shows different packets; each row corresponds to a different packet called a **frame**
1. No.	Number of packets in the current live/offline capture

Item	What is it?
2. Time	Shows time-stamped information when the packet was captured The **Automatic** setting for `libpcap` files is microseconds; all packets will be captured with the time in microseconds, as shown in the next screenshot
3. Source	The IP address of the source from where the packet originates
4. Destination	The IP address of the destination where the packet ends
5. Protocol	Wireshark will display information about the packet protocol based on the standard port
6. Length	The packet length in bytes
7. Info	Shows a high-level summary of the packet and the nature of the packet

To change the time-stamped information of the packet go to **View | Time Display Format** to view the available presentation formats, as shown:

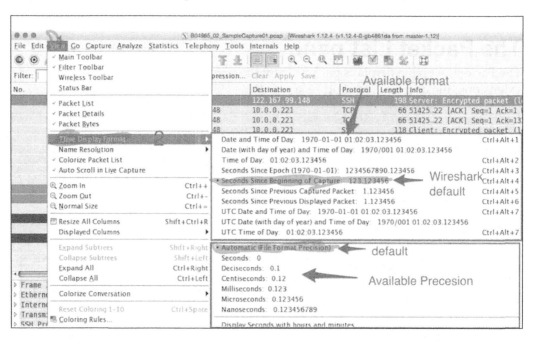

The Wireshark **Set Time Reference** feature gives you the ability to view the time reference from the selected packet. Open the capture file `http.pcap` and set the time reference from packet 38. To do this, select packet 38, right-click, and select **Set Time Reference (toggle)**, as shown in the following screenshot:

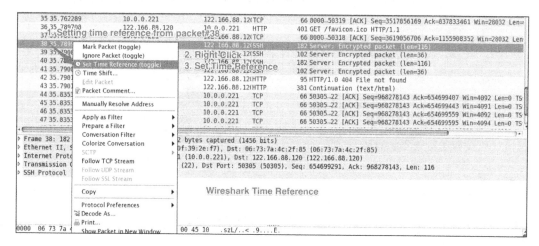

After *REF* is set, it becomes the starting point for all subsequent packet time calculations, as shown in the following screenshot:

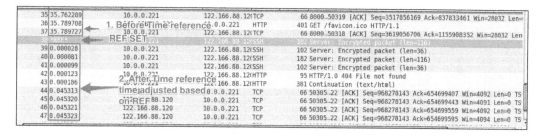

The Packet Details pane

The Packet Details pane will show the currently selected packet in a more detailed form. In the following screenshot, an HTTP packet is selected and its details are shown in the information labeled with numbers **1** to **5**. Let's see what these are:

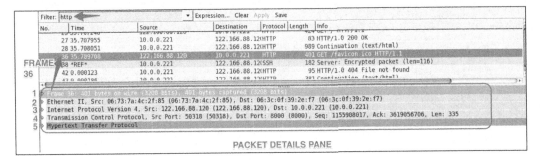

PACKET DETAILS PANE

The frame protocol is only used by Wireshark. All the TCP/IP protocols sits on top of this. The frame shows at what time the packet was captured, as shown in the following screenshot:

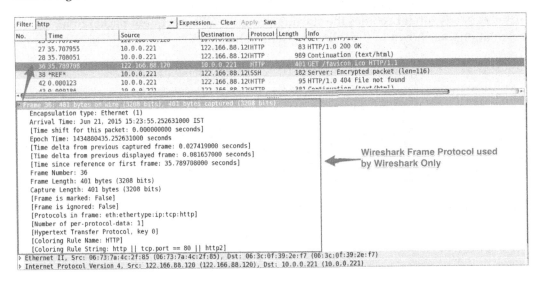

Ethernet is the link layer protocol in the TCP/IP stack. It sends network packets from the sending host to one (Unicast) or more (Multicast/Broadcast) receiving hosts, as shown:

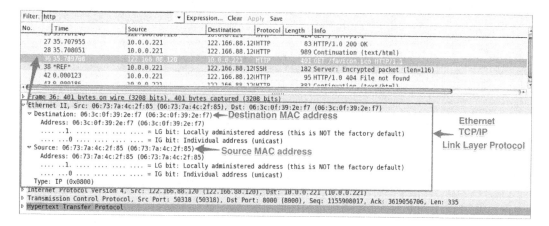

Useful filters in Ethernet are:

- `eth.dst == 06:3c:0f:39:2e:f7`: This shows packets sent to this MAC address only

- `eth.dst==ff:ff:ff:ff:ff:ff`: This shows broadcast traffic only

The packet structure of Ethernet frames is described in the following table:

Preamble	Destination MAC address	Source MAC address	Type/length	User-data	Frame check sequence (FCS)
8	6	6	2 0800 for IPv4 86DD for IPv6 0806 for ARP	46-1500	4

The preamble (8 bytes) and FCS (4 bytes) are not part of the frame and Wireshark will not capture this field.

So the total Ethernet header is 14 bytes—6 bytes for the destination address, 6 bytes for the source address, and 2 bytes for the EtherType.

The Internet Protocol information relates to how the IP packet is delivered and whether it has used IPv4 or IPv6 to deliver the datagram packets.

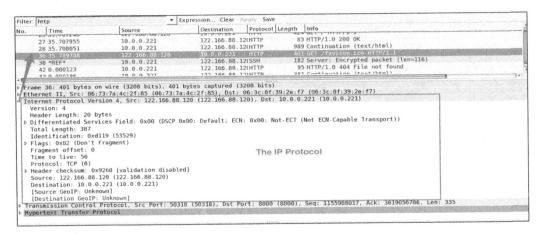

The preceding screenshots show that an IPv4 protocol is used to deliver the datagram packet. Useful display filters in the IP protocol are:

- `ip.src == 122.166.88.120/24` shows traffic from the subnet
- `ip.addr==122.166.88.120` shows traffic to or from the given host
- Host `122.166.88.120` captures/filters traffic from the host

The TCP protocol packet contains all TCP-related protocol data. If the communication is over UDP, the TCP will be replaced by the UDP, as shown in the following screenshot. The SEQ/ACK analysis will be done by Wireshark based on the sequence number and expert info will be provided:

The <<APPLICATION-LAYER>> protocol is shown if the packet contains any application protocols. As shown in the following screenshot, the selected packet 36 has HTTP protocol data. Wireshark has the ability to decode the protocol based on the standard port and present this information in the Packet Details pane in a readable (RFC-defined) format.

In the coming chapters we will discuss the application-related protocol in greater detail.

The Packet Bytes pane

The Packet Bytes pane displays the bytes contained in the frame, with the highlighted area being set to the node selected in the Packet Details pane.

Wireshark features

Wireshark is loaded with some awesome features. Let's go through a few, though there are more.

Decode-As

The Decode-As feature allows Wireshark to decode the packet based on the selected protocol. Usually Wireshark will automatically identify and decode incoming packets based on the standard port—for example, port 443 will be decoded as SSL. If the services are running on the non-standard port, for example SSL standard port is 443 and the service is running on 4433, in this case the Decode-As feature can be used to decode this communication using the SSL protocol preference.

Open the sample `https.pcap` file from. HTTPS traffic is captured when the file is opened in Wireshark. It doesn't show SSL-related data; instead it just shows all TCP communications:

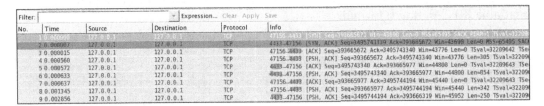

To decode this traffic as SSL, follow these steps:

1. Click on **Analyze | Decode As**:

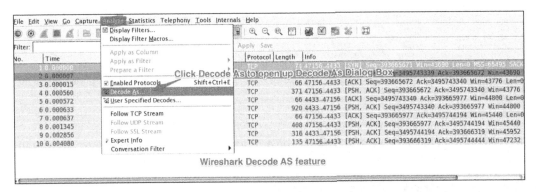

Wireshark Decode AS feature

2. The **Decode As** popup will appear as shown in the following screenshot. Choose the protocol (**SSL** in this example) that is required for decoding the given traffic:

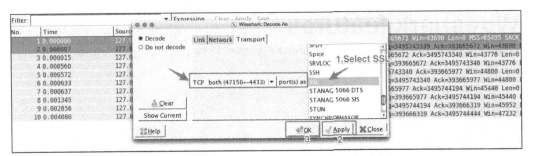

3. The SSL traffic protocol is shown in Wireshark:

Filter:		▾	Expression... Clear Apply Save		SSL Handshake & Application Data shown	
No.	Time	Source	Destination	Protocol	Length	Info
1 0.000000	127.0.0.1	127.0.0.1	TCP		74 47156..4433 [SYN] Seq=393665671 Win=43690 Len=0 MSS=65495 SACK
2 0.000007	127.0.0.1	127.0.0.1	TCP		74 4433..47156 [SYN, ACK] Seq=3495743339 Ack=393665672 Win=43690
3 0.000015	127.0.0.1	127.0.0.1	TCP		66 47156..4433 [ACK] Seq=393665672 Ack=3495743340 Win=43776 Len=0
4 0.000560	127.0.0.1	127.0.0.1	TLSv1.2		371 Client Hello
5 0.000572	127.0.0.1	127.0.0.1	TCP		66 4433..47156 [ACK] Seq=3495743340 Ack=393665977 Win=44800 Len=0
6 0.000633	127.0.0.1	127.0.0.1	TLSv1.2		920 Server Hello, Certificate, Server Hello Done
7 0.000637	127.0.0.1	127.0.0.1	TCP		66 47156..4433 [ACK] Seq=393665977 Ack=3495744194 Win=45440 Len=0
8 0.001345	127.0.0.1	127.0.0.1	TLSv1.2		408 Client Key Exchange, Change Cipher Spec, Encrypted Handshake N
9 0.002856	127.0.0.1	127.0.0.1	TLSv1.2		316 New Session Ticket, Change Cipher Spec, Encrypted Handshake Me
10 0.004080	127.0.0.1	127.0.0.1	TLSv1.2		135 Application Data

[SSL decoding doesn't mean it has decrypted the SSL data.]

Protocol preferences

The protocol preference feature provides the flexibility for you to customize how the Wireshark display is processed, and how packets are analyzed. You can set protocol preferences by one of the following methods:

- Go to **Edit | Preferences | Protocols** to adjust the settings
- A simple way is to right-click on a protocol in the Packet Details pane and select **Protocol Preferences**

Wireshark supports a large set of protocols and it's preferences, for example HTTP protocol preferences and their meanings as defined in the following table:

HTTP protocol preferences	What does this mean?
Reassemble HTTP headers spanning multiple TCP segments	HTTP dissector will reassemble the HTTP header if it has been transmitted over more than one TCP segment
Reassemble HTTP bodies spanning multiple TCP segments	HTTP dissector will reassemble the HTTP body if it has been transmitted over more than one TCP segment
Reassemble chunked transfer-coded bodies	Reassemble all chunks across the segments and add them to the payload
Decompress entity bodies	Used for the visualization of compressed data (.gzip or encoded)
SSL/TLS ports	Add/remove SSL/TLS ports (default is 443)
Custom HTTP header fields	Define new header fields

The following screenshot shows HTTP protocol preferences in Wireshark:

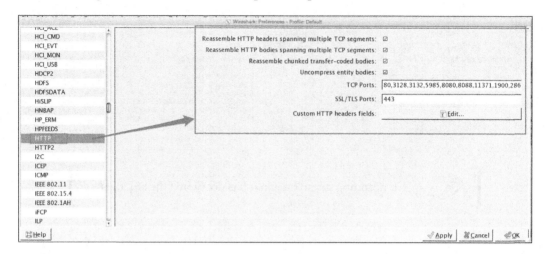

 Refer to the example of finding the top HTTP response time in *Chapter 05, Analyze the DHCP, DHCPv6, DNS, HTTP Protocols* when using protocol preferences.

The IO graph

Use the IO graph to check client and server interaction data for a meaningful analysis. The Wireshark IO graph measures throughput (the rate is packet-per-tick), where each tick is one second. In this example we will see how to make use of the IO graph. Open the file http_01.pcap in Wireshark and follow the given steps:

1. Click on **Statistics | IO graph**.
2. The **IO graph** dialog box will appear.
3. In the **IO graph** dialog box try to find the spike and click on it.
4. When you click on the graph (the high area), Wireshark will automatically show the corresponding packet in the Packet List pane.

 In the given example there are lots of duplicate ACKs.

5. Go back to the **IO graph** dialog box.

6. Choose **Graph2** and enter `tcp.analysis.duplicate_ack`.

7. Click on **Graph2** to apply the filter.

8. The **IO graph** dialog will show the throughput of the duplicate ACK.

There are a lot of use cases for IO graphs. Some of them are as follows:

- Use IO graphs to analyze traffic patterns, for example how the traffic is distributed by plotting graphs on protocols for example `tcp`, `http`, `udp`, `ntp`, and `ldap`.

- IO graphs come in handy when performing security analysis. More examples of IO graphs are available in *Chapter 07, Network Security Analysis*.

The following screenshots show the results of the preceding steps:

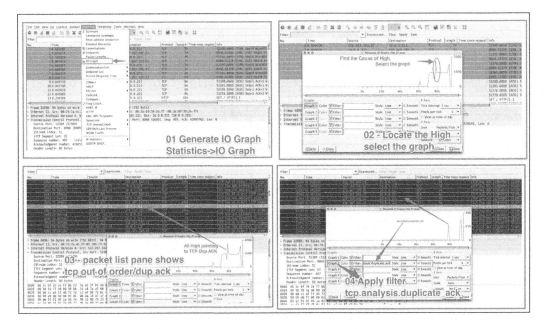

Following the TCP stream

The TCP stream feature allows users to see the data from a TCP stream. Open the file `http_01.pcap` in Wireshark and follow the TCP stream to get the first HTTP OK, as shown:

In this example we have located the HTTP OK on packet#35 and then right clicked and selected **Follow TCP Stream**:

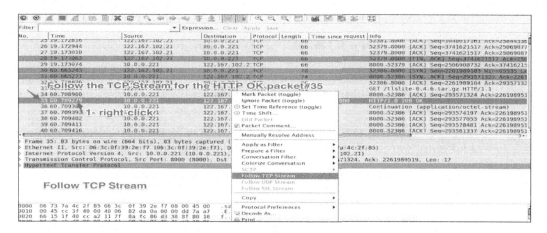

Once the stream is applied, a TCP stream dialog box will open displaying which request is sent and what response is received in this HTTP conversation:

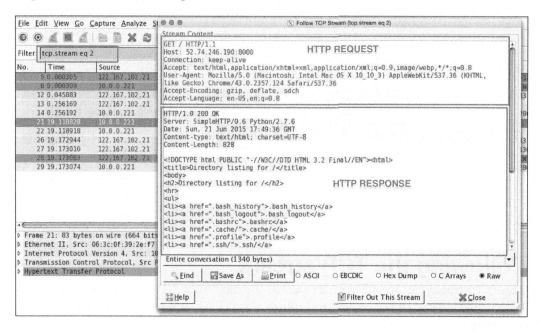

The stream content is available in six formats as shown; the red content in the screenshot is the request, the blue content in the screenshot is the response:

Exporting the displayed packet

The **Export Specified Packets** feature allows you to export the filtered packet in different files. For example, open `http.pcap` in Wireshark and export the HTTP OK packet. The steps for exporting a specified packet are as follows:

1. Apply the filter `http.response.code == 200` in the **Filter** bar:

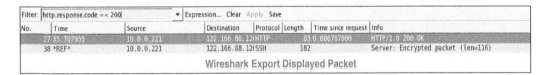

2. Go to **File | Export Specified Packets**. This opens up the dialog box with the export options, as shown:

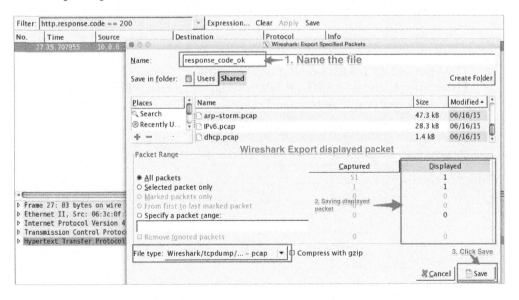

Generating the firewall ACL rules

Using Wireshark, network administrators can generate ACL rules for firewall products such as:

- Cisco IOS
- IP Filter (ipfilter)
- IP Firewall (ipfw)
- Netfilters (iptables)
- Packet Filter (pf)
- Windows Firewall (netsh)

 Rules for MAC addresses and IPv4 addresses are present; the filter supports TCP, UDP ports, and IPv4 port combinations.

The steps to generate an ACL rule in Wireshark are as follows:

1. Go to **Tool | Firewall ACL Rules**:

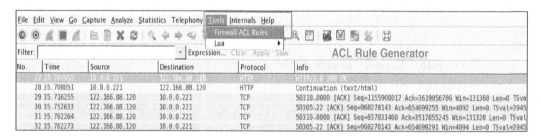

2. The **Firewall ACL Rules** dialog box will appear. Choose **Product** and **Filter**, specify the **ACCEPT/DENY** criteria, and a rule will be generated by Wireshark in this dialog box, as shown:

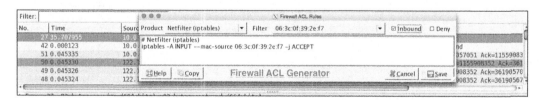

Tcpdump and snoop

In production environments, packet-capturing tools such as Wireshark are usually not installed. In such scenarios, a default-capturing tool can be used such as `tcpdump` for (Linux systems) and `snoop` (the Solaris default); later the captured file can be used in Wireshark for analysis:

- `snoop`: This tool captures and inspects network packets and runs on Sun Microsystems CLI
- `tcpdump`: This tool dumps traffic on a network and runs on Windows, OS X, and Linux

For example, the following table shows how to check packets from interfaces:

Description	Solaris	Linux
How to check packets from all interfaces	`bash# snoop`	`bash#tcpdump -nS`
How to capture with hostname	`bash# snoop hostname`	`bash# tcpdump host hostname`
How to write the captured information to a file	`snoop -o filename`	`bash# tcpdump -w filename`
How to capture packets between `host1` and `host2` and save them to a file	`snoop -o capture_file.pcap host1 host2`	`tcpdump -w capture_file.pcap src host1 and dst host2`

How to capture traffic with verbose output to screen	`snoop -v -d eth0`
	
	`snoop -d eth0 -v port 80`
		`tcpdump -i eth0`
		
		Very Verbose `tcpdump` options:
		
		`tcpdump -i eth0 -v port 80`
		
		`tcpdump -i eth0 -vv port 80`

How to set the snaplength	`snoop -s 500`	`tcpdump -s 500`
How to capture all bytes	`snoop -s0`	`tcpdump -s0`
How to capture the IPv6 traffic	`snoop ip6`	`tcpdump ip6`

Description	Solaris	Linux

How to capture protocols	`snoop multicast`
	`snoop broadcast`
	`snoop bootp`
	`snoop dhcp`
	`snoop dhcp6`
	`snoop pppoe`
	`snoop ldap`
		`tcpdump -n "broadcast or multicast"`
		`tcpdump udp`
		`tcpdump tcp`
		`tcpdump port 67`
		`tcpdump port 546`
		`tcpdump port 389`

References

You can also refer to the following links for more information on the topics covered in this chapter:

- `https://www.wireshark.org/docs/wsug_html_chunked/`
- `https://wiki.wireshark.org/CaptureSetup/Ethernet`
- `https://goo.gl/vxI2jk`

Summary

In this chapter we have learned how to use the Wireshark GUI. Then we explored what capture filters and display filters are, how to set up a capture, keeping performance in mind, and how to make use of other capturing tools such as `tcpdump` and `snoop` in production or in remote capturing. Then we learned about a few Wireshark features such as ACL rule generation, IO graph, Decode-As, exporting packets, and protocol preferences.

In the next chapter we will learn the TCP protocol and will discuss its practical use cases with a lab exercise that will help in troubleshooting common network problems (we will also provide the solution).

Analyzing the TCP Network 3

TCP is intended to be a host-to-host protocol in common use in multiple networks. In this chapter, we will analyze the TCP protocol in detail with lab exercises and examples.

This chapter covers the following topics:

- Recapping TCP
- TCP connection establishment and clearing
- TCP troubleshooting
- TCP latency issues
- Wireshark TCP sequence analysis

Recapping TCP

Transmission Control Protocol (TCP) was first defined in RFC 675, and the v4 specification came out in RFC 793. TCP provides:

- Connection-oriented setup and tear-down of TCP sessions
- The service sends and receives a stream of bytes, not messages, and guarantees that all bytes received will be identical with bytes sent and in the correct order
- Reliable, in-order delivery, uses sequence number to recover from data that is damaged, lost, duplicated, or delivered out of order by the Internet communication system
- Flow control prevents the receiver's buffer space from overflowing
- Congestion control (as defined in RFC 5681) algorithms are: slow start, congestion avoidance, fast retransmit, and fast recovery
- Multiplexing; every TCP conversation has two logical pipes; an outgoing and incoming pipe

TCP header fields

Each TCP segment has a 20-byte header with optional data values, as shown in the following screenshot displaying a TCP frame in the Wireshark Packet Details pane:

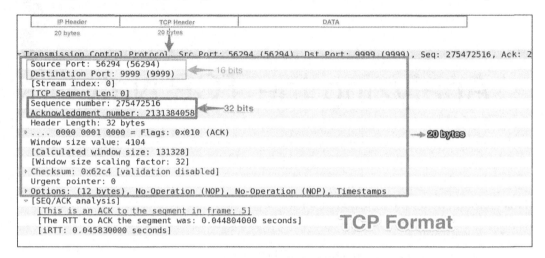

The following table describes the header fields and Wireshark filters along with their descriptions:

TCP header	Wireshark filter name	Description
Source port (16 bits)	`tcp.srcport`	Sender port
Destination port (16 bits)	`tcp.dstport`	Receiver port
Sequence Number (32 bits)	`tcp.seq`	Defines the ISN and controls the state of the TCP
Acknowledgement number (32 bits)	`tcp.ack`	The ACK contains the next SEQNo that a host wants to receive

TCP header		Wireshark filter name	Description
Flags (9 bits)		`tcp.flags`	Control bits
	Reserved	`tcp.flags.res`	For future use
	Nonce	`tcp.flags.ns`	Experimental
	CWR	`tcp.flags.cwr`	Congestion window reduced
	ECN	`tcp.flags.ecn`	ECN-Echo
	Urgent	`tcp.flags.urg`	Urgent pointer field is set
	Acknowledgement	`tcp.flags.ack`	Acknowledgement is set
	Push	`tcp.flags.push`	Push the data
	Reset	`tcp.flags.reset`	Reset the connection
	SYN	`tcp.flags.syn`	Synchronize sequence numbers
	FIN	`tcp.flags.fin`	No more data
Window size (16 bits)		`tcp.window_size`	Used to advertise the window size in a three-way handshake
Checksum (16 bits)		`tcp.checksum`	Error checking
Urgent pointer (16 bits)		`tcp.urgent_pointer`	Inform the receiver that some data in the segment is *urgent* (SEQNo <= urgent message <= SEQNo + urgent pointer)
Options (0-132 bits) divisible by 32		`tcp.options`	Options such as maximum segment size, **No-Operation** (**NOP**), window scale, timestamps, SACK permitted

TCP states

A connection progresses through a series of states during its lifetime. The states are:

TCP state	Description
LISTEN	The server is open for incoming connection.
SYN-SENT	The client has initiated the connection.
SYN-RECEIVED	The server has received the connection request.
ESTABLISHED	The client and server are ready for the data transfer, a connection has been established.

FIN-WAIT-1	The client or server has closed the socket. In Linux the default is 60 ms:
	`[bash ~]# cat /proc/sys/net/ipv4/tcp_fin_timeout`
	`60`

TCP state	Description

FIN-WAIT-2	The client or server has released the connection. In Linux the default is 60 ms:
	
	`[bash ~]# cat /proc/sys/net/ipv4/tcp_fin_timeout`
	`60`

CLOSE-WAIT	Either client or server has not closed the socket. The CLOSE_WAIT state will not expire.
LAST-ACK	Waiting for pending ACK from the client. It's the final stage of the TCP conversation with the client.

TIME-WAIT	TIME_WAIT indicates that the local application closed the connection, and the other side acknowledged and sent a FIN of its own. In Linux the default is 60 ms:
	
	`[bash ~]# cat /proc/sys/net/ipv4/tcp_fin_timeout`
	`60`

CLOSED	Fictional state

This socket command-line utility can be used to monitor network connections and their states:

```
[bash ~]ss -nt4 state CLOSE-WAIT
[bash ~]ss -nt4 state ESTABLISHED
[bash ~]netstat -an | grep CLOSE-WAIT
[bash ~]netstat -an | grep ESTABLISHED
```

TCP connection establishment and clearing

In this section we will learn how the TCP opens and closes its connections. In order to establish a connection, the three-way handshake procedure is used as described in the following section.

TCP three-way handshake

The three-way handshake is a connection establishment procedure from the client socket to the server socket, as shown in the following image:

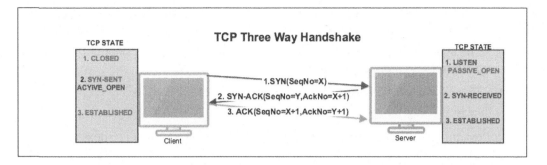

Before the start of the TCP three-way handshake, the client will be in the CLOSED state and the server will be in the LISTEN state as shown:

SN	TCP-A (122.167.84.137)		FLOW CTL	TCP-B(10.0.0.221)	
	STATE			**STATE**	
	FROM	**TO**		**FROM**	**TO**
1	CLOSED			CLOSED	LISTEN

The TCP state machine

To examine a three-way handshake in Wireshark, open the `normal-connection.pcap` file provided in the book.

Handshake message – first step [SYN]

The first step of the handshake process is that the socket client will construct a SYN packet and send it to the server. During this process the socket client will perform the following tasks:

1. `tcp.flags.syn` is set to `1` and its SYN packet is sent by the client.
2. The client generates and sets the `tcp.seq=3613047129` the **initial sequence number (ISN)**. Wireshark shows, by default, relative sequence numbers; a user can change this setting under: **Edit | Preferences | Protocols | TCP | Relative sequence numbers**.
3. The client sets `tcp.ack =0`.
4. The `tcp.window_size` is advertised to the server and its value is in the packet `tcp.window_size_value == 65535`, which tells it that it can transmit up to `65535` bytes of data depending on MSS. For example if MSS is 1440 bytes, the client can transmit 45 segments.

5. TCP client includes other `tcp.options` such as **Maximum Segment Size (MSS)**, **No-Operation (NOP)**, window scale, timestamps, and SACK permitted.

6. The client chooses `tcp.options.sack_perm == 1` in the "selective acknowledgements" processing.

• TSval/TSecr is the timestamp `tcp.options.timestamp.tsval == 123648340`.

The following table depicts the state transition of the first handshake message:

Sr. No.	TCP-A (122.167.84.137) state		Flow CTL	TCP-B (10.0.0.221) state	
	From	**To**		**From**	**To**
1	CLOSED			CLOSED	LISTEN
2	CLOSED	SYN_SENT	<SEQ=3613047129><CTL=SYN>	LISTEN	

TCP state machine changes SYN_SENT

Handshake message – second step [SYN, ACK]

In this process the server responds to the client's SYN:

1. The server sets `tcp.flags.syn =1` and `tcp.flags.ack=1`, confirming that the SYN has been accepted.

2. The server generates and sets ISN `tcp.seq=2581725269`.

3. The server sets `tcp.ack=3613047130` as the client `tcp.seq+1`.

4. The server sets `tcp.window_size_value == 26847` as the server window size.

5. The server sets `tcp.options` and responds to the client.

The following table depicts the state transitions of the second handshake message:

Sr. No.	TCP-A (122.167.84.137) state		Flow CTL	TCP-B (10.0.0.221) state	
	From	**To**		**From**	**To**
1	CLOSED			CLOSED	LISTEN
2	CLOSED	SYN_ SENT	<SEQ=3613047129><CTL=SYN>	LISTEN	
3	SYN_ SENT		<SEQ=2581725269><ACK=3613 047130><CTL=SYN,ACK>	LISTEN	SYN-RECEIVED

TCP state machine changes when SYN-RECEIVED is sent by the server

Handshake message – third step [ACK]

After successfully exchanging this message, the TCP connection will be established in this connection:

1. The client sets `tcp.flags.ack == 1` and sends to the server.

2. The client `tcp.seq=3613047130` is ISN+1 and `tcp.ack=2581725270` is `SYN_ACK( tcp.seq+1)`.

3. The client window size is set again and this will be used by the server `tcp.window_size_value == 4105`.

 `tcp.analysis.flags` shows you packets that have some kind of expert message from Wireshark.

The following table depicts the state transitions of the third handshake message:

Sr. No.	TCP-A (122.167.84.137) state		FLOW CTL	TCP-B(10.0.0.221) state	
	From	To		From	To
1	CLOSED			CLOSED	LISTEN
2	CLOSED	SYN_SENT	<SEQ=3613047129><CTL=SYN>	LISTEN	
3	SYN_SENT		<SEQ=2581725269><ACK=3613047130><CTL=SYN,ACK>	LISTEN	SYN-RECEIVED
4	SYN_SENT	ESTABLISHED	<SEQ=3613047130>><ACK=2581725270><CTL=ACK>	SYN-RECEIVED	ESTABLISHED

TCP state machine when the client sends ACK

TCP data communication

Once the three-way connection is established, the data is communicated by exchanging the segments and the PUSH flag is set to indicate that the data flows on a connection as a stream of octets, as shown in the following figure:

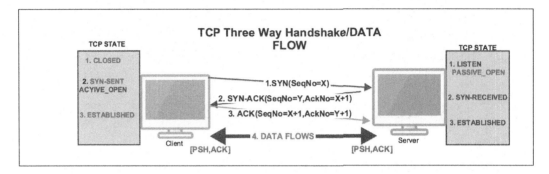

Select **packet#4** from the `normal-connection.pcap` file as shown in the following screenshot; expand the TCP section in the Packet Details pane:

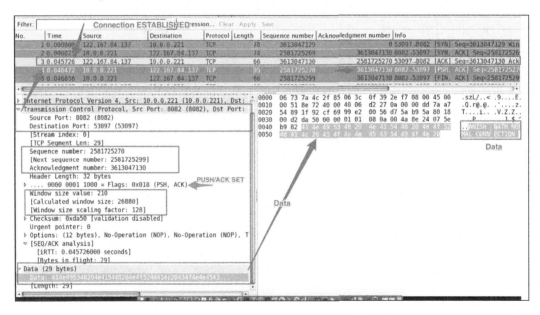

As you can see in the preceding screenshot:

1. The server is sending data to the client as shown in the packet.
2. The server sets `tcp.flags.push = 1`.
3. The server sets `tcp.flags.ack =1`.
4. The server data is (29 bytes) and the data value is:
   `414e495348204e415448204e4f524d414c20434f4e4e4543....`
5. The server sets `(tcp.flags.ack == 1) && (tcp.flags.push == 1)`; that is, the `[PSH,ACK]` flag indicates that the host is acknowledging receipt of some previous data and also transmitting some more data.

The useful Wireshark display filters are:

- `data`: Displays the packet that contains the data information, for all IPs:

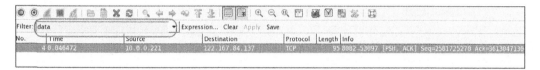

- `data && ip.addr==10.0.0.221`: Displays a list of packets that have data and are exchanged with the given IP address
- `tcp.flags.push == 1`: Displays all PUSH packets
- `tcp.flags.push == 1 && ip.addr==10.0.0.221`: Displays PUSH packets between hosts
- `tcp.flags == 0x0018`: Display all PSH, ACK packets
- `tcp.flags == 0x0011`: Displays all FIN, ACK packets
- `tcp.flags == 0x0010`: Displays all ACK packets

TCP close sequence

TCP normal close appears when the client or server decides that all data has been sent to the receiver and we can close the connection. There are three ways a TCP connection is closed:

- The client initiates closing the connection by sending a FIN packet to the server
- The server initiates closing the connection by sending a FIN packet to the client

- Both client and server initiate closing the connection

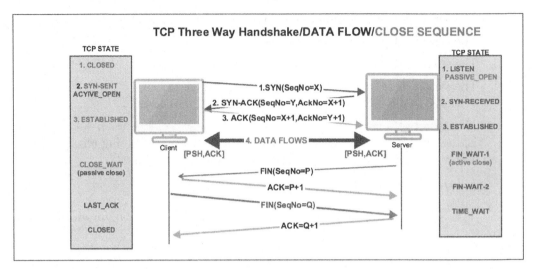

Open the `normal-connection.pcap` file and select packet #5 in the Packet List pane. Go to the Wireshark Packet Details pane, as shown in the screenshot, and examine the TCP protocol.

In Wireshark add the **Sequence number** and **Acknowledgement number** to the column. To add the sequence number and acknowledgement number, choose the TCP header packet, right-click on the field (**Sequence number / Acknowledgement number**) in the packet details and select **Display as Column**. Or implement these settings to add a new column:

- Go to **Edit | Preferences | Columns**. Then add a new column and select "**custom**" : tcp.seq.

- Go to **Edit | Preferences | Columns**. Then add a new column and select "**custom**" : tcp.ack.

The server has initiated the FIN packet. When the data transfer is completed, see packet#5 in the following screenshot:

No.	Time	Source	Destination	Sequence number	Acknowledgment number	Info
1	0.000000	122.167.84.137	10.0.0.221	3613047129	0	53097→8082 [SYN] Seq=3613047129 Win=6553!
2	0.000025	10.0.0.221	122.167.84.13	2581725269	3613047130	8082→53097 [SYN, ACK] Seq=2581725269 Ack=
3	0.045726	122.167.84.137	10.0.0.221	3613047130	2581725270	53097→8082 [ACK] Seq=3613047130 Ack=25817
4	0.046472	10.0.0.221	122.167.84.13	2581725270	3613047130	8082→53097 [PSH, ACK] Seq=2581725270 Ack=
5	0.046656	10.0.0.221	122.167.84.13	2581725299	3613047130	8082→53097 [FIN, ACK] Seq=2581725299 Ack=
6	0.100657	122.167.84.137	10.0.0.221	3613047130	2581725299	53097→8082 [ACK] Seq=3613047130 Ack=25817
7	0.100668	122.167.84.137	10.0.0.221	3613047130	2581725300	53097→8082 [ACK] Seq=3613047130 Ack=25817
8	0.100675	122.167.84.137	10.0.0.221	3613047130	2581725300	53097→8082 [FIN, ACK] Seq=3613047130 Ack=
9	0.100683	10.0.0.221	122.167.84.13	2581725300	3613047131	8082→53097 [ACK] Seq=2581725300 Ack=36130

As you can see in the preceding screenshot:

- The server initiates the `FIN` packet to close the connection in packet#5
- The server set `[FIN,ACK]` `(tcp.flags.fin == 1) && (tcp.flags.ack == 1)` and sends it to the client
- The server sequence number `tcp.seq == 2581725299` is acknowledged in packet#7
- The client is initiating `FIN` to close the connection in packet#8
- The client sets `[FIN,ACK]` `(tcp.flags.fin == 1) && (tcp.flags.ack == 1)` and sends it to the server
- The client sequence number `tcp.seq == 3613047130` is acknowledged in packet#9

The TCP state machine when the server and client close the socket connection, server initiated `FIN`:

Sr. No.	TCP-A (122.167.84.137) State		Flow CTL	TCP-B(10.0.0.221) State	
	From	To		From	To
1	CLOSED			CLOSED	LISTEN
2	CLOSED	SYN_SENT	<SEQ=3613047129><CTL=SYN>	LISTEN	
3	SYN_SENT		<SEQ=2581725269><ACK=3613047130><CTL=SYN,ACK>	LISTEN	SYN-RECEIVED
4	SYN_SENT	ESTABLISHED	SEQ=3613047130>><ACK=2581725270><CTL=ACK>	SYN-RECEIVED	ESTABLISHED
5	ESTABLISHED	ESTABLISHED	<SEQ=3613047130>><ACK=2581725270><CTL=PSH,ACK>	ESTABLISHED	ESTABLISHED
6	ESTABLISHED	ESTABLISHED	<SEQ=3613047130>><ACK=2581725299><CTL=ACK>	ESTABLISHED	ESTABLISHED
7	ESTABLISHED	ESTABLISHED	<SEQ=2581725299>><ACK=3613047130><CTL=FIN.ACK>	ESTABLISED	FIN_WAIT-1
8	ESTABLISHED	CLOSE_WAIT	<SEQ=3613047130>><ACK=2581725300><CTL=ACK>	FIN_WAIT-1	FIN_WAIT-2
9	CLOSE_WAIT	LAST_ACK	SEQ=3613047130>><ACK=2581725300><CTL=FIN.ACK>	FIN_WAIT-2	TIME_WAIT
10	LAST_ACK	CLOSED		TIME_WAIT	CLOSED

Wireshark filters used in this scenario are as follows:

- `tcp.analysis:SEQ/ACK`: Provides links to the segments of the matching sequence/ack numbers
- `tcp.connection.fin`: Provides expert information
- `tcp.flags == 0x0011`: Displays all the `[FIN,ACK]` packets

Lab exercise

The steps to capture the normal TCP connection flow (a sample program is provided as part of this book) are as follows:

1. Open Wireshark, start capturing the packets, and choose display filter `tcp.port==8082`.

2. Compile the Java program `TCPServer01.java` using the `javac` command:

   bash$ ~ javac TCPServer01.java

3. Run `TCPServer01` using the `java` command:

   bash$ ~ java TCPServer01

4. Verify the server is listening on port `8082`:

   bash$ ~ netstat -an | grep 8082

   tcp46   0   0 *.8082   *.*
                            LISTEN

5. Compile the client program `Client0301.java` using the `javac` command:

   bash$ ~ javac Client0301.java

6. Run the client program:

   bash$ ~ java Client0301

7. View and analyze the packet in Wireshark.

TCP troubleshooting

In this section we will learn about different network problems that occur and try to analyze and solve them with lab exercises. Let's start with the `Reset` (`RST`) packet.

TCP reset sequence

The TCP RST flag resets the connection. It indicates that the receiver should delete the connection. The receiver deletes the connection based on the sequence number and header information. If a connection doesn't exist on the receiver RST is set, and it can come at any time during the TCP connection lifecycle due to abnormal behavior. Let's take one example: a RST packet is sent after receiving SYN/ACK, as shown in the next image.

RST after SYN-ACK

In this example we will see why RST has been set after SYN-ACK instead of ACK:

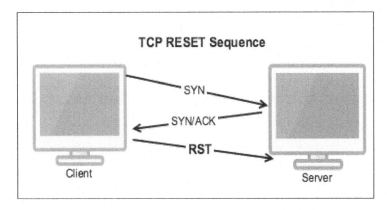

Open the RST-01.pcap file in the Wireshark:

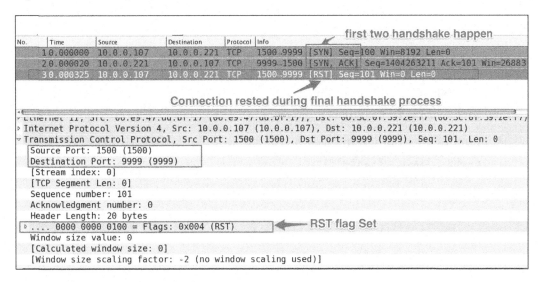

As you can see in the preceding figure:

- The TCP RST packet should not be seen normally
- The TCP RST is set after the first two handshakes are complete. A possible explanation could be one of the following:
  - ° The client connection never existed; a RAW packet was send over the TCP server
  - ° The client aborted its connection
  - ° The sequence number got changed/forged

RST after SYN

This is the most common use case. Open the RST-02-ServerSocket-CLOSED.pcap file in Wireshark. In this example the server was not started, the client attempted to make a connection, and the connection refused an RST packet:

```
1 0.000000  122.167.84.13 10.0.0.221   TCP   51685-9999 [SYN] Seq=787188611 Win=65535 Len=0 MSS=1440
2 0.000036  10.0.0.221    122.167.84.   TCP   9999-51685 [RST, ACK] Seq=0 Ack=787188612 Win=0 Len=0
```

RST is set Immediately after SYN recieved

```
▷ Frame 1: 78 bytes on wire (624 bits), 78 bytes captured (624 bits)
▷ Ethernet II, Src: 06:73:7a:4c:2f:85 (06:73:7a:4c:2f:85), Dst: 06:3c:0f:39:2e:f7 (06:3c:0f:39:2e:f7)
▷ Internet Protocol Version 4, Src: 122.167.84.137 (122.167.84.137), Dst: 10.0.0.221 (10.0.0.221)
▷ Transmission Control Protocol, Src Port: 51685 (51685), Dst Port: 9999 (9999), Seq: 787188611, Len: 0
```

Lab exercise

The steps to generate the RST flag in a generic scenario, when the server is not in the listening state, are as follows:

1. Open Wireshark, start capturing the packets, and choose display filter tcp.port==8082.

2. Compile the client program Client0301.java:

   bash$ ~ javac Client0301.java

3. Run the client program:

   bash$ ~ java Client0301

4. View and analyze the RST packet in Wireshark.

TCP CLOSE_WAIT

Often a connection is stuck in the CLOSE_WAIT state. This scenario typically occurs when the receiver is waiting for a connection termination request from the peer.

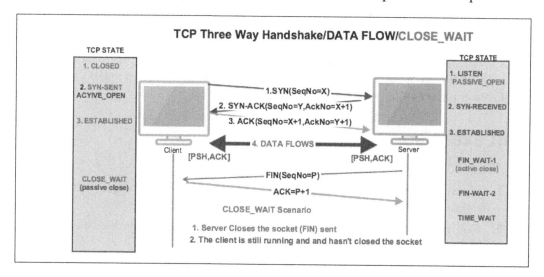

To find a socket in the CLOSE_WAIT state, use the following commands:

```
bash:~ $ netstat -an | grep  CLOSE_WAIT
tcp4       0       0 122.167.127.21.56294
10.0.0.21.9999     CLOSE_WAIT
```

To demonstrate the CLOSE_WAIT state, open the close_wait.pcap file in Wireshark:

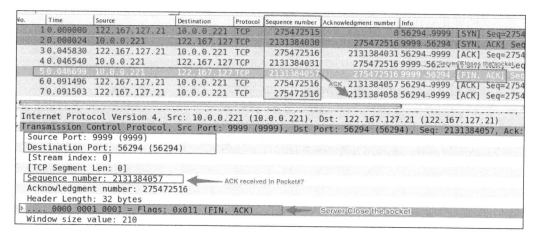

As you can see in the preceding screenshot:

1. The server closed socket packet#5, set `tcp.flags.fin == 1`, and set `tcp.seq == 2131384057`.

2. The client responded with the ACK packet `tcp.ack == 2131384058` in packet#7 and didn't close its socket, which remains in the CLOSE_WAIT state.

CLOSE_WAIT means there is something wrong with the application code, and in the high-traffic environment if CLOSE_WAIT keeps increasing, it can make your application process slow and can crash it.

Lab exercise

The steps to reproduce CLOSE_WAIT are as follows:

1. Open Wireshark, start capturing the packets, and choose display filter `tcp.port==9999`.

2. Compile the Java programs `Server0302.java` and `Client0302.java` using the `javac` command:

   ```
   bash$ ~ javac Server0302.java Client0302.java
   ```

3. Run `Server0302` using the `java` command:

   ```
   bash$ ~ java TCPServer01
   ```

4. Verify the server is listening on port 9999:

   ```
   bash $ netstat -an | grep 999
   tcp46      0       0  *.9999                    *.*
                               LISTEN
   ```

5. Run the client program:

   ```
   bash$ ~ java Client0302
   ```

6. Check the state of the TCP socket; it will be in the CLOSE_WAIT state:

   ```
   bash $ netstat -an | grep CLOSE_WAIT
   tcp4       0       0  127.0.0.1.56960
           127.0.0.1.9999             CLOSE_WAIT
   ```

7. Analyze the packet in Wireshark.

How to resolve TCP CLOSE_STATE

The steps are as follows:

1. To remove CLOSE_WAIT, a restart is required for the process.

2. Establishing the FIN packet from both the client and server is required to solve the CLOSE_WAIT problem. Close the client socket and server socket when done with processing the record:

    ```
    socket.close(); à Initiates the FIN flow
    ```

3. Open the Client0302.java file and close the socket:

    ```
    Socket socket = new Socket(InetAddress.getByName
      ("localhost"), 9999);

    ...

    socket.close();

    ...

    Thread.sleep(Integer.MAX_VALUE);
    ```

4. Compile and re-run the Java program. CLOSE_WAIT will not be visible.

TCP TIME_WAIT

The main purpose of the TIME_WAIT state is to close a connection gracefully, when one of ends sits in LAST_ACK or CLOSING retransmitting FIN and one or more of our ACK are lost.

RFC 1122: *"When a connection is closed actively, it MUST linger in TIME-WAIT state for a time 2xMSL (Maximum Segment Lifetime). However, it MAY accept a new SYN from the remote TCP to reopen the connection directly from TIME-WAIT state, if..."*

We ignore the conditions because we are in the TIME_WAIT state anyway.

TCP latency issues

Until now we have been troubleshooting connection-related issues. In this section, we will check the latency part. Latency can be on the network, or in application processing on the part of the client or server.

Cause of latency

Identifying the source of latency also plays an important role in TCP troubleshooting. Let's see what the common causes of latency are:

- Network slow wire latency can be measured with the `ping` utility
- Too many running processes eat memory. Check the memory management, work with free, top command to identify CPU and memory use
- Application not started with sufficient memory or cannot serve more requests
- Bad TCP tuning; verify the `/etc/sysctl.cnf` file
- Network jitter; verify your network and check with the network administrator
- Poor coding; benchmark your code by performing a load test over the network
- Gateway wrongly set; check the gateway, verify the routing table, and verify the gateway
- Higher hop counts; do a traceroute and check the number of hops (the higher the hop count, the more latency increases)
- Slow NIC interface, the interface goes down; check the NIC card and verify its speed

Identifying latency

Various network utility tools are available to measure the latency between networks — for example `traceroute`, `tcpping`, and `ping`.

- `ping`: This utility can be used to measure the **round trip time (RTT)**:

```
bash$ ping -c4 google.com
PING google.com (216.58.196.110): 56 data bytes
64 bytes from 216.58.196.110: icmp_seq=0 ttl=55 time=226.034 ms
64 bytes from 216.58.196.110: icmp_seq=1 ttl=55 time=207.748 ms
64 bytes from 216.58.196.110: icmp_seq=2 ttl=55 time=222.995 ms
64 bytes from 216.58.196.110: icmp_seq=3 ttl=55 time=162.507 ms

--- google.com ping statistics ---
4 packets transmitted, 4 packets received, 0.0% packet loss
round-trip min/avg/max/stddev = 162.507/204.821/226.034/25.394 ms
```

- `traceroute`: This is used to identify the number of HOPS it has taken to reach the destination — the fewer the hops, the lower the latency

Server latency example

Wireshark can be used effectively to identify whether the network is slow or the application is slow. Open the `slow_download.pcap` file in Wireshark, and investigate the root cause of why the download is slow.

In this example, 5 MB of data is requested from the HTTP server, and it has taken approx. 4.99 minutes to download, as shown:

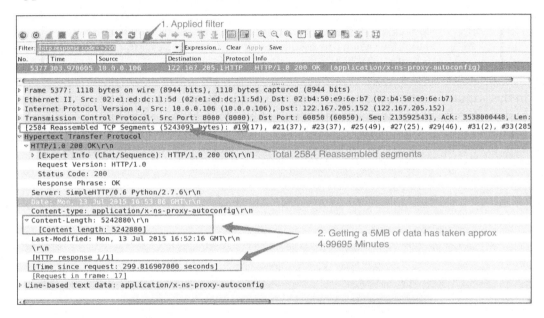

The steps to diagnose this issue are as follows:

1. Go to **Edit | Preferences | Protocols | HTTP** and then enable all HTTP reassemble options.

2. Apply the filter `http.response.code==200`.

3. Go to **HTTP** and set the `http.time == 299.816907000` to approximately 4.99 minutes.

4. Check the size of the file by navigating to `http.content_length_header == "5242880"`; this is the size of the content.

5. Check how many TCP segments have been sent— `tcp.segment.count == 2584` —and ask yourself whether so many are needed and whether the number can be reduced.

6. Verify `window_size` for the client and server to check what was advertised by the client and what got used.

7. Add `tcp.window_size_value` in the **Wireshark** column and sort in ascending order. Note that the entire packet flow from the server (`10.0.0.16`) to the client (`122.167.205.152`) has a window size of `100`.

8. Verify the `sysctl.conf` file in UNIX-flavored systems and check the TCP tuning parameters such as `net.core.rmem_max`, `net.core.wmem_max`, `net.ipv4.tcp_rmem`, and `net.ipv4.tcp_wmemnet.ipv4.tcp_mem`.

 Make sure `tcp.window_size` stays large enough to avoid slowing down the sender. The window size can tell you if a system is too slow when processing incoming data; `tcp_window_size` indicates that the system is slow, not the network.

In this scenario, `tcp.window_size` was reduced in the `sysctl.conf` file to demonstrate the `slow_download` behavior and to give an insight into troubleshooting. After fixing `Window_Size`, the same download is reduced from `299.816907000` to `2.84` seconds. Open the `fast_download.pcap` file as shown in the following screenshot; the download time is reduced:

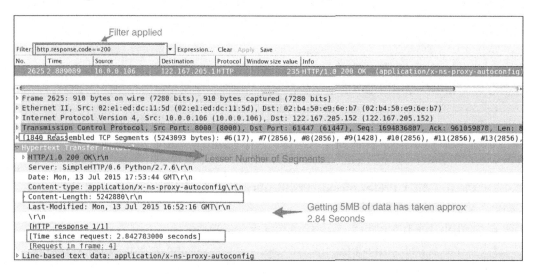

Wire latency

In this example, the TCP handshake process will be used to identify wire latency. Open the `slow_client_ack.pcap` file as shown in the following screenshot:

No.	Time	Source	Destination	Protocol	Info
1	0.000000	10.0.0.107	10.0.0.221	TCP	59459→9999 [SYN] Seq=1375307982 Win=26883 Len=0 MSS=8961 SACK_PE
2	0.000568	10.0.0.221	10.0.0.107	TCP	9999→59459 [SYN, ACK] Seq=3612770469 Ack=1375307983 Win=26847 Le
3	15.798777	10.0.0.107	10.0.0.221	TCP	59459→9999 [ACK] Seq=1375307983 Ack=3612770470 Win=27008 Len=0 T
4	15.801537	10.0.0.221	10.0.0.107	TCP	9999→59459 [PSH, ACK] Seq=3612770470 Ack=1375307983 Win=26880 Le
5	15.801555	10.0.0.107	10.0.0.221	TCP	59459→9999 [ACK] Seq=1375307983 Ack=3612770507 Win=27008 Len=0 T
6	27.946811	10.0.0.107	10.0.0.221	TCP	59459→9999 [FIN, ACK] Seq=1375307983 Ack=3612770507 Win=27008 Le
7	27.948950	10.0.0.221	10.0.0.107	TCP	9999→59459 [FIN, ACK] Seq=3612770507 Ack=1375307984 Win=26880 Le
8	27.948963	10.0.0.107	10.0.0.221	TCP	59459→9999 [ACK] Seq=1375307984 Ack=3612770508 Win=27008 Len=0 T

Time Since reference

```
▷ Frame 1: 74 bytes on wire (592 bits), 74 bytes captured (592 bits)
▷ Ethernet II, Src: 06:e9:47:dd:bf:17 (06:e9:47:dd:bf:17), Dst: 06:3c:0f:39:2e:f7 (06:3c:0f:39:2e:f7)
▷ Internet Protocol Version 4, Src: 10.0.0.107 (10.0.0.107), Dst: 10.0.0.221 (10.0.0.221)
▷ Transmission Control Protocol, Src Port: 59459 (59459), Dst Port: 9999 (9999), Seq: 1375307982, Len: 0
```

As you can see in the preceding screenshot:

- The first two handshake messages (SYN, SYN-ACK) sent by the client/server over the wire are exchanged in less time

- In the last handshake message, ACK sent by the client has taken `frame.time_relative == 15.798777000` seconds and shows an increase in **Time Since Reference**. This is higher than the first two handshake messages, which confirms a wire latency on this packet

- Once the handshake is completed, the operation resumes normally; the Time Since reference for all packets shows a consistent timing

Wireshark TCP sequence analysis

Wireshark has a built-in filter, `tcp.analysys.flags`, that will show you packets that have some kind of expert message from Wireshark; `tcp.analysis.flags` is shown in the **TCP** section of the **Packet Details** pane. Under that, expand **SEQ/ACK analysis** then expand **TCP Analysis Flags**. This will tell you exactly what triggered `tcp.analysis.flags`. A few examples include:

- TCP Retransmission
- TCP Fast Retransmission
- TCP DupACK
- TCP ZeroWindow
- TCP ZeroWindowProbe

TCP retransmission

TCP makes the transmission of segments reliable via sequence number and acknowledgement. When TCP transmits a segment containing data, it puts a copy on a retransmission queue and starts a timer; when the acknowledgment for that data is received, the segment is deleted from the queue. If the acknowledgment is not received before the timer runs out, the segment is retransmitted. During TCP retransmission, the sequence number is not changed until the retransmission timeout happens.

Open the example `tcp-retransmission.pcapng` in Wireshark and add a **Sequence number** column, as shown in the following screenshot:

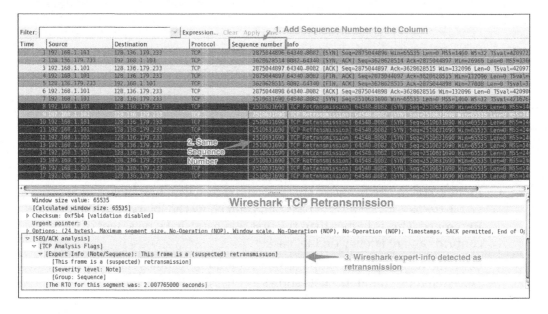

As you can see in the preceding screenshot:

- After sending `tcp.seq == 1870089183` a lot of TCP retransmission occurs
- A lot of TCP Retransmission can result in operation timeouts

For another example, open the file `syn_sent_timeout_SSH.pcapng` in Wireshark, and observe the TCP retransmission flow.

KeepAlive is not a retransmission.

Lab exercise

The steps to reproduce the TCP retransmission are as follows (this lab is performed in CentOs6 using the `telnet` and `nc` command utilities):

1. Set up two machines: HOST-A (Server) and HOST-B (client).

2. On HOST-A start the server and configure the firewall rule as shown:

   ```
   [bash ~]# iptables -A OUTPUT -p tcp --dport 8082 -j DROP
   [bash ~]# iptables save
   [bash ~]# nc -l 8082
   ```

3. On the HOST-B machine open Wireshark, start capturing the packets, and choose display filter `tcp.port==8082`.

4. On the HOST-B machine run the telnet command; change the IP information to your actual server location:

   ```
   [bash ~]telnet 128.136.179.233 8082
   ```

5. Verify the TCP state on the HOST-B machine:

   ```
   bash$ netstat -an |   grep 8082
   tcp4       0       0  192.168.1.101.64658
      128.136.179.233.8082    SYN_SENT
   ```

6. In Wireshark, view and analyze the captured packet using the previous step.

In order to solve operation timeouts, verify the ACL configuration; it allows the incoming packet from the source IP.

TCP ZeroWindow

Open the `tcp_zero_window.pcapng` file in Wireshark and add `tcp.window_size_value` to the column.

The TCP window size represents how much data a device can handle from its peer at one time before it is passed to the application process.

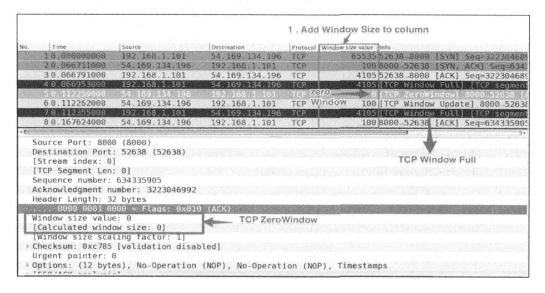

As shown in the preceding screenshot:

- Add `window_size` to the Wireshark column and look for the packet where `tcp.window_size=0`.

- TCP headers with a window size of zero indicate that the receiver's buffers are full. This condition arrives more rapidly for writes than reads; in this condition `tcp.window_size_value` is set to `0` and `tcp.window_size == 0`.

- The segment is exactly 1 byte.

 SYN/RST/FIN flags are never set on TCP ZeroWindow.
SYN/RST/FIN flags are never set on TCP Window Full.

Troubleshoot the ZeroWindow condition:

- Check the application has sufficient memory to start with
- Tune the TCP parameters to obtain a larger window size; check the `sysctl.conf` file with these parameters:
    - `net.core.rmem_max`
    - `net.core.wmem_max`

- ° `net.ipv4.tcp_rmem`
- ° `net.ipv4.tcp_wmem`

- Check the receiver is not running too many processes

TCP Window Update

Wireshark marks a packet as Window Update when the window size has changed. A Window Update is an ACK packet, and only expands the window; this is normal TCP behavior.

Open the `tcp_window_update.pcap` file in Wireshark and observe that a TCP Window Update event is set, as shown:

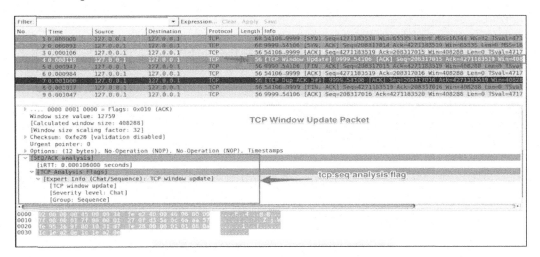

 A Window Update is a 0-byte segment with the same SEQ/ACK numbers as the previously seen segment and with a new window value.

TCP Dup-ACK

Duplicate ACKs are sent when there is fast retransmission. In this scenario the same segment will be seen often. Open `duplicate_ack.pcapng` and apply the `tcp.analysis.duplicate_ack` filter, as shown:

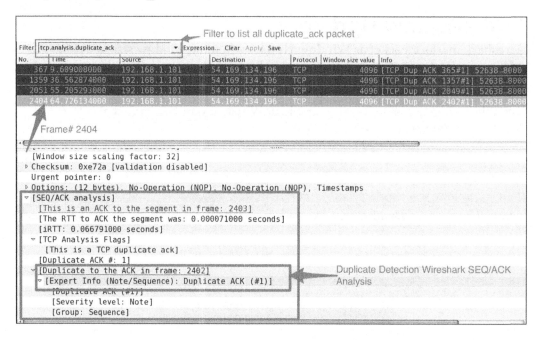

As you can see in the previous screenshot:

- Duplicate ACKs occur when the Window/SEQ/ACK is the same as the previous segment and if the segment length is 0

- Duplicate ACKs can occur when there is a packet loss, in which case a retransmission can be seen

References

The following references will be useful while working with TCP/IP not limited:

- RFC675 TCP/IP first specification: `https://tools.ietf.org/html/RFC675`

- RFC793 TCP v4: `https://tools.ietf.org/html/RFC793`

- TCP Wiki: `https://en.wikipedia.org/wiki/Transmission_Control_Protocol`

- The TCP/IP guide at: `http://www.tcpipguide.com/`

- Ask Wireshark for all Wireshark-related queries at: `https://ask.wireshark.org/`

- Display filter references for TCP at: `https://www.wireshark.org/docs/dfref/t/tcp.html`

- TCP analyze sequence numbers at: `https://wiki.wireshark.org/TCP_Analyze_Sequence_Numbers`

- Helpful clips at: `https://goo.gl/1VaEc9`

Summary

In this chapter you have learnt how the TCP opens and closes its connection, and how TCP states are maintained during this period. This chapter also covered error patterns seen on networks and how to troubleshoot those scenarios.

In the next chapter we will implement deep-packet inspections of the SSL protocol.

4
Analyzing SSL/TLS

In this chapter we will learn what SSL/TLS is used for, how the entire handshake process happens, and about the common areas where the SSL/TLS handshake fails, by covering the following topics:

- An introduction to SSL/TLS
- The SSL/TLS Handshake Protocol with Wireshark
- SSL/TLS — decrypting communication with Wireshark
- SSL/TLS — debugging handshake issues

An introduction to SSL/TLS

Transport Layer Security (TLS) is the new name for **Secure Socket Layer (SSL)**. It provides a secure transport connection between applications with the following benefits:

- SSL/TLS works on Layer 7 (the Application Layer) on behalf of the higher-level protocols
- SSL/TLS provides confidentiality and integrity by encrypting communications
- SSL/TLS allows client-side validation (optional) for closed use cases

SSL/TLS versions

Knowing the versions is extremely important while debugging handshake issues, as most handshake failures happen in this process.

Netscape developed the original SSL versions and other versions; their RFC numbers are shown in the following table:

Protocol	Year	RFC	Deprecated
SSL 1.0	N/A	N/A	N/A
SSL 2.0	1995	NA	Y RFC 6176
SSL 3.0	1996	RFC 6101	Y RFC 7568
TLS 1.0	1999	RFC 2246	N
TLS 1.1	2006	RFC 4346	N
TLS 1.2	2008	RFC 5246	N
TLS 1.3	TBD	DRAFT	N

The SSL/TLS component

SSL/TLS is split into four major components, as shown in the following screenshot, and this chapter will cover all components in detail, one by one:

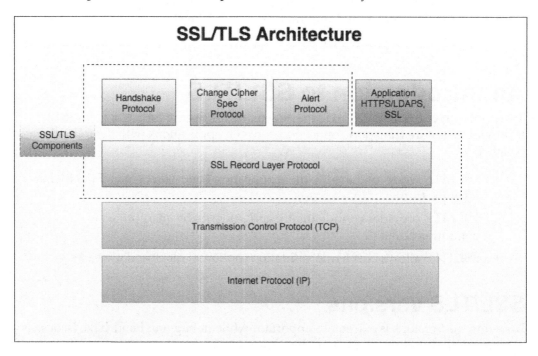

The SSL/TLS handshake

The TLS Handshake Protocol is responsible for the authentication and key exchange necessary to establish or resume a secure session. Handshake Protocol manages the following:

- Client and server will agree on cipher suite negotiation, random value exchange, and session creation/resumption
- Client and server will arrive at the pre-master secret
- Client and server will exchange their certificate to verify themselves with the client (optional)
- Generating the master secret from the pre-master secret and exchanging it

Types of handshake message

There are ten types of message, as shown in the following table, and their corresponding Wireshark filters. This is a one-byte field in the Handshake Protocol:

Type	Protocol	Message	Wireshark content type	Wireshark filter
0	Handshake	Hello request	ssl.record.content_type == 22	ssl.handshake.type == 0
1		Client Hello		ssl.handshake.type == 1
2		Server Hello		ssl.handshake.type == 2
11		Certificate		ssl.handshake.type == 11
12		ServerKeyExchange		ssl.handshake.type == 12
13		CertificateRequest		ssl.handshake.type == 13
14		ServerHelloDone		ssl.handshake.type == 14
15		Certificate Verify		ssl.handshake.type == 15
16		Client Key Exchange		ssl.handshake.type == 16
20		Finished		ssl.handshake.type == 20

Type	Protocol	Message	Wireshark content type	Wireshark filter
	ChangeCipherSpec		`ssl.record.content_type == 20`	
	Application Data		`ssl.record.content_type == 23`	
	Alert Protocol		`ssl.record.content_type == 21`	

The TLS Handshake Protocol involves the following steps in four phases; the prerequisite is that a TCP connection should be established:

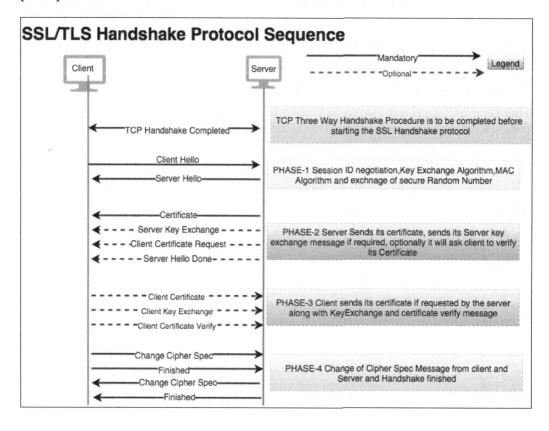

Open the file `two-way-handshake.pcap`, which is an example demonstrating a SSL mutual authentication procedure:

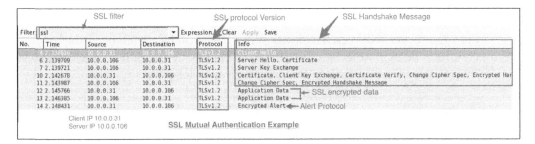

Client Hello

The TLS handshake starts with the Client Hello message (`ssl.handshake.type == 1`), as shown in the following screenshot:

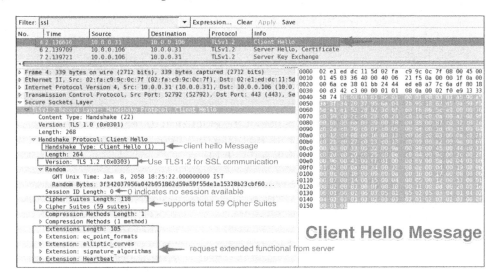

Handshake records are identified as hex byte `0x16=22`. The structure of the Client Hello message is as follows:

- **Message**: The Client Hello message `0x01`.

- **Version**: The hex byte `0x0303` means it's TLS 1.2; note `0x300 =SSL3.0`.

- **Random**:
    - `gmt_unix_time`: The current time and date in standard UNIX 32-bit format
    - `Random bytes`: 28 bytes generated by the secure random number

- **Session ID**: The hex byte `0x00` shows the session ID as empty; this means no session is available and generates new security parameters.

- **Cipher suites**: The client will provide a list of supported cipher suites to the server; the first cipher suite in the list is the client-preferred (the strongest) one. The server will pick the cipher suites based on its preferences, the only condition being that the server must have client-offered cipher suites otherwise the server will raise an alert/fatal message and close the connection:

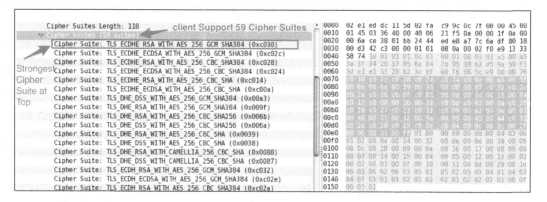

- **Compression methods**: The client will list the compression methods it supports.

- **Extensions**: The client makes use of the extension to request extended functionality from the server; in this case the client has requested four extensions, as shown in the following table:

Value	Extension name	Reference
0	elliptic_curve	RFC4492
1	ec_point_formats	RFC4492
3	signature_algorithms	RFC 5246
5	heartbeat	RFC 6520

 For a complete list of TLS extensions, visit: http://www.iana.org/assignments/tls-extensiontype-values/tls-extensiontype-values.xhtml.

Server Hello

The server will send the Server Hello message (`ssl.handshake.type == 2`) in response to the Client Hello, as shown in the following screenshot. The message structure of the Client Hello and Server Hello message is the same, with one difference — the server can select only one cipher suite:

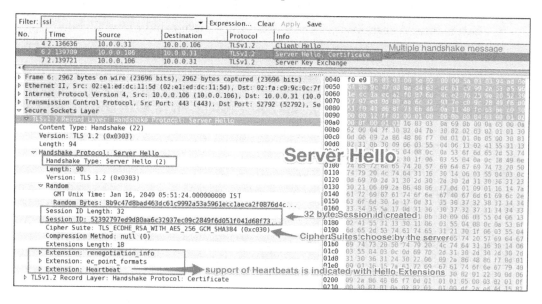

Handshake records are identified as hex byte `0x16=22`. The structure of the Server Hello message is:

- **Handshake Type**: The hex byte `0x02=2` shows the Server Hello message
- **Version**: The hex byte `0x0303` shows TLS 1.2 has been accepted by the server

The following table shows which SSL version of the client can connect to which SSL version of the server:

Server/client	SSLv2	SSLv3	SSLv23	TLSv1	TLSv1.1	TLSv1.2
SSLv2	Y	N	Y	N	N	N
SSLv3	N	Y	Y	N	N	N
SSLv23	N	Y	Y	Y	Y	Y
TLSv1	N	N	Y	Y	N	N
TLSv1.1	N	N	Y	N	Y	N
TLSv1.2	N	N	Y	N	N	Y

- **Session ID**: A 32-byte session ID is created for reconnection purposes without a handshake

- **Cipher suite**: The server has picked `Cipher Suite: TLS_ECDHE_RSA_WITH_AES_256_GCM_SHA384 (0xc030)`, which means use **Elliptic curve Diffie-Hellman (ECDHE)** key exchange, RSA for authentication, Block cipher Galois/Counter Mode (GCM), AES-256 for encryption, and SHA-384 for digests

- **Extensions**: A response with extension info is requested in the Client Hello message

Server certificate

After the Server Hello message is sent, the server should send a X.509 server certificate (`ssl.handshake.type == 11`). The certificate configured on the server are signed by the CA or intermediate CA, or can be self-signed based on your deployment:

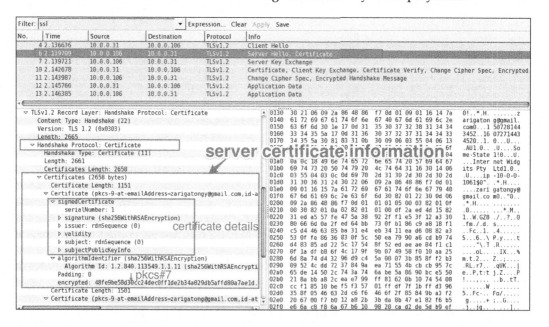

If a SSL/TLS server is configured with the certificate chain then the entire chain will be presented to the client along with the server certificate. The client (a browser or any other SSL/TLS client) can then check the highest certificate in the chain with stored CA certificates; typically, modern Web browsers have the root CA installed from the trusted CA provider.

The given certificate is signed with the relevant signature (`sha256WithRSAEncryption`); in this case, the hash value itself is concatenated into the OID (`Algorithm Id: 1.2.840.113549.1.1.11`) representing the signing algorithm. The certificate follows the DER encoding format and when encrypted becomes PKCS#7, the Cryptographic Message Syntax Standard (refer to RFC 2315).

Server Key Exchange

From RFC #5246, the server sends the Server Key Exchange message (`ssl.handshake.type == 12`) only when the Server Certificate message (if sent) does not contain enough data to allow the client to exchange a premaster secret:

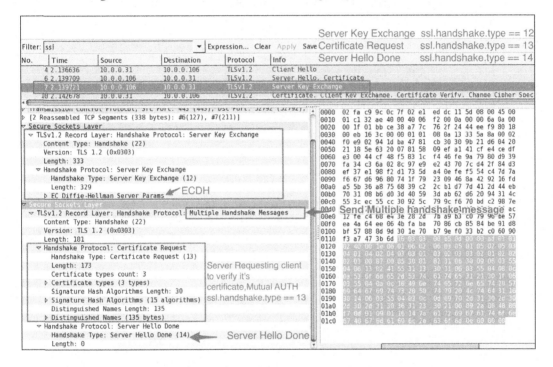

As you can see in the preceding screenshot:

- Cipher suites contains key exchange algorithms
- The Server Key Exchange message will be sent for the following key exchange methods: DHE_DSS, DHE_RSA, DH_anon
- In line with RFC#5246, the use of Server Key Exchange is not legal for these key exchange methods: RSA, DH_DSS, DH_RSA

Client certificate request

The server can optionally ask client to verify its certificate. To support mutual authentication, the server will send the certificate request message (`ssl.handshake. type == 13`) to the client and the client must provide its certificate information to the server. If the client fails to provide it, an Alert protocol will be generated and the connection will terminate.

Server Hello Done

The Server Hello Done message means that the server is done sending messages to support the key exchange, and the client can proceed with its phase of the key exchange:

```
▽ Secure Sockets Layer
    ▽ TLSv1.2 Record Layer: Handshake Protocol: Server Hello Done
        Content Type: Handshake (22)
        Version: TLS 1.2 (0x0303)
        Length: 4
      ▽ Handshake Protocol: Server Hello Done
          Handshake Type: Server Hello Done (14)      Server Hello Done
          Length: 0
```

Client certificate

The client will send its certificate (`ssl.handshake.type == 11`) only in a mutual authentication condition. The server will verify the certificate in its CA chain. If the server fails to verify `client_certificate`, the server will raise an alert fatal protocol and communication will stop:

Client Key Exchange

In the case of the normal handshake process (one way auth), the Client Key Exchange message is the first message sent by the client after it receives the Server Hello Done message.

This Client Key Exchange message (`ssl.handshake.type == 16`) will always be sent by the client. When this message is seen, `pre_master_secret` is set, either by transmission of the RSA-encrypted secret or by the Diffie-Hellman parameters, depending on the key exchange method chosen. The server uses its private key to decrypt `premaster_secret`:

Client Certificate Verify

The Client Certificate Verify message will be sent after the Client Key Exchange message (`ssl.handshake.type == 16`) using `master_secret` generated by `pre_master_secret`.

Change Cipher Spec

The Change Cipher Spec record type (`ssl.record.content_type == 20`) is different from the handshake record type (`ssl.record.content_type == 22`) and it's a part of the Change Cipher Spec protocol. The Change Cipher Spec message is sent by both the client and server only when `key_exchange` is completed and it indicates to the receiving party that subsequent records will be protected under the newly negotiated Change Cipher Spec and keys (`master_secret`):

Finished

The Finished (`ssl.record.content_type == 22`) message is encrypted so it will be an **encrypted handshake message** in Wireshark. This message is sent immediately after a Change Cipher Spec message from both the client and server to verify that the key exchange and authentication processes were successful. This message contain the MD5 hash +SHA hash. When both the client and server have sent the Finished message, the TLS handshake is considered to have finished successfully and now sending and receiving application data over the secure channel can begin:

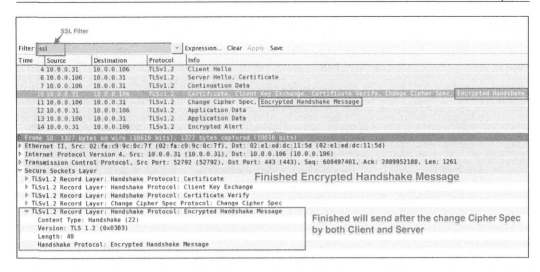

Application Data

The Application Data message (`ssl.record.content_type == 23`) is carried by the record layer and fragmented, compressed, and encrypted:

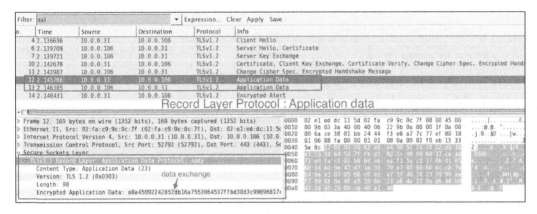

Record layer processing involves the mentioned step as shown in the following screenshot:

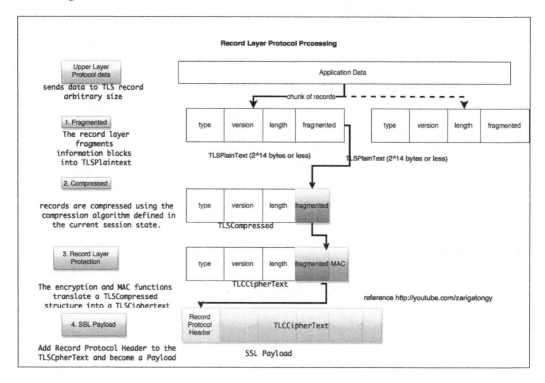

Alert Protocol

The Alert Protocol (`ssl.record.content_type == 21`) describes the severity of the message and the alert. Alert messages are encrypted and compressed and support two alert levels: warning and fatal. In the case of fatal alerts, the connection will be terminated.

Alert descriptions are shown in the following table:

Alert name	Alert type	Description
close_notify(0)	Closure alert	Sender will not send any more messages on this connection
unexpected_message(10)	Fatal	An inappropriate message was received
bad_record_mac(20)	Fatal	Incorrect MAC received
decryption_failed(21)	Fatal	TLS Cipher text decrypted in an invalid way
record_overflow(22)	Fatal	Message size is more than $2^{14}+2048$ bytes

Alert name	Alert type	Description
decompression_failure(30)	Fatal	Invalid input received
handshake_failure(40)	Fatal	Sender unable to finalize the handshake
bad_certificate(42)	Fatal	Received corrupted certificate; bad ASN sequence
unsupported_certificate(43)	Fatal	Certificate type is not supported
certificate_revoked(44)	Warning	Signer has revoked the certificate
certificate_expired(45)	Warning	The certificate is not valid
certificate_unknown(46)	Warning	Certificate unknown
illegal_parameter(47)	Fatal	TLV contain invalid parameters
unknown_ca(48)	Fatal	CA chain couldn't be located
access_denied(49)	Fatal	Certificate is valid, the server denied the negotiation
decode_error(50)	Fatal	The TLV received does not have a valid form
decrypt_error(51)	Fatal	Decryption cipher invalid
export_restriction(60)	Fatal	A negotiation not in compliance with export restrictions was detected
protocol_version(70)	Fatal	The selected protocol version is not supported by the server
insufficient_security(71)	Fatal	Strong cipher suite needed
internal_error(80)	Fatal	Server-related issue
user_canceled(90)	Fatal	Client cancelled the operation
no_renegotiation(100)	Fatal	Server is not able to negotiate the handshake

As shown in the following screenshot, the Alert Protocol is generated by the server:

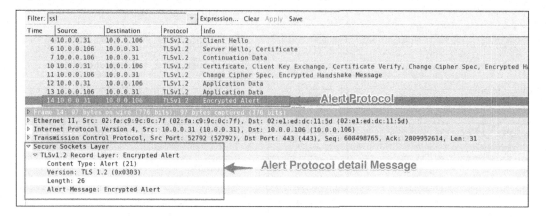

Key exchange

In the next section, we will talk about how the SSL/TLS channel can be decrypted; before that, we need to understand what the different keys exchange methods are and what their cipher suites look like. These are the following key exchange methods.

The Diffie-Hellman key exchange

This protocol allows two users to exchange a secret key over an insecure medium without any prior secrets; in this scheme, the example cipher suites will have a naming convention such as:

- SSL_DH_RSA_WITH_DES_CBC_SHA
- SSL_DH_RSA_WITH_3DES_EDE_CBC_SHA

Cipher suites will have "DH" in their name, not "DHE" or "DH_anon".

 You can learn more about Diffie-Hellman at: `https://en.wikipedia.org/wiki/Diffie-Hellman_key_exchange`.

Elliptic curve Diffie-Hellman key exchange

Elliptic curve Diffie-Hellman is a modified Diffie-Hellman exchange that uses elliptic curve cryptography instead of the traditional RSA-style large primes. **Elliptic curve cryptography** (ECC) is a public-key cryptosystem just like RSA, Rabin, and El Gamal. Some important points with this algorithm are:

- Every user has a public and a private key
- The public key is used for encryption/signature verification
- The private key is used for decryption/signature generation

 You can learn more about Elliptic Curve Diffie-Hellman at: `https://en.wikipedia.org/wiki/Elliptic_ curve_Diffie-Hellman`.

Note that the Client Hello message exchange process in the Extension elliptic_curves key exchange was offered. The example cipher suites will follow a naming convention such as:

- SSL_DHE_RSA_WITH_DES_CBC_SHA
- SSL_DHE_RSA_WITH_3DES_EDE_CBC_SHA

Cipher suites will have "DHE" in their name, not "DH" or "DH_anon".

RSA

The server's public key is made available to the client during the Server Key Exchange handshake. The `pre_master_secret` key is encrypted with the server public RSA key. The example cipher suites in this case will be:

- SSL_RSA_WITH_RC4_128_SHA
- SSL_RSA_WITH_DES_CBC_SHA
- TLS_RSA_WITH_AES_128_CBC_SHA

Cipher suites will have "RSA" in their name, not "DH" or "DH_anon" or "DHE".

Decrypting SSL/TLS

So far we have learned how the SSL/TLS protocol encrypts traffic and maintains confidentiality. In the next section, we will cover how Wireshark helps to decrypt SSL/TLS traffic.

Decrypting RSA traffic

Decryption of TLS traffic depends upon which cipher suite was chosen by the server in the Server Hello message. Open the file `decrypt-ssl-01.pcap` and look for the cipher selected by the server. In this case the TLS_RSA_WITH_AES_256_CBC_SHA cipher suite was used; since this is RSA, we can decrypt the packet using our private key.

Now go to **Edit | Preferences | Protocol | SSL**, add the new RSA key, and configure the following properties of the RSA key dialog box:

1. The Private key file (here, `server.key`, which is used by the server).
2. The IP address of the server.
3. The port of the SSL/TLS server (`443`).
4. The decoding protocol — use `http` in this case.

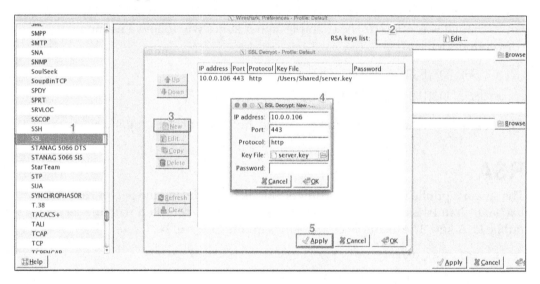

After applying these settings, the SSL traffic will be decoded into HTTP traffic for that IP, as shown in the following screenshot:

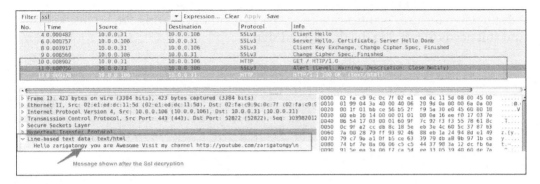

Message shown after the Ssl decryption

Once the packet is decrypted, the SSL session can be exported by clicking on **File | Export SSL Session Keys**. A dialog box will open; save this session key in the file (`exported-session-keys`). The content of the file looks like this:

```
RSA Session-ID:af458c9c61675238b74f40b2a9547a0a2a394ada458a1b648e0495ed27
9d5e2e Master-Key:6c970211a77548811267646a759d0d03bbc532d9b6336f2b656cb0c
6bbef8f3a262d845b9abed87d26583a9c4bb9b230
```

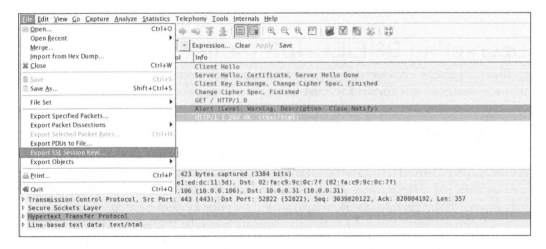

Once the `exported-session-keys` file is created, use this file to decrypt the SSL/TLS traffic. To do so, go to **Edit | Preferences | Protocol | SSL** and configure the (Pre)-master-secret log file with the path of the SSL Session Keys. This approach is helpful when the user wants to share the packet without sharing the private keys and still needs to provide the decryption step:

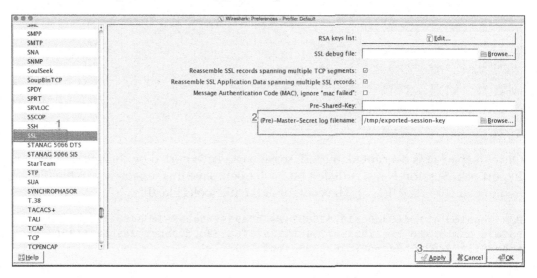

Decrypting DHE/ECHDE traffic

DHE/ECDHE can't be decrypted using this approach even if we have private keys as they are designed to support forward secrecy.

Forward secrecy

Forward secrecy is supported in the **Diffie-Hellman (DHE)** and **Elliptic curve cryptography Diffie-Hellman (ECDHE)** key exchange algorithms. Take the previous scenario; the SSL/TLS communication can be decrypted by knowing the server's private key. If the private key is compromised by poor system hardening or (an internal threat agent), the SSL/TLS communication can be broken. In forward secrecy, the SSL/TLS communication is secure even if we have access to the server's private key.

If the cipher suite's name contains "ECDHE" or "DHE", it means it supports forward secrecy. For example, note this cipher suite name: TLS_ECDHE_RSA_WITH_RC4_128_SHA.

Some useful references for this are as follows:

- `http://security.stackexchange.com/ questions/35639/decrypting-tls-in-wireshark- when-using-dhe-rsa-ciphersuites/42350#42350`
- `https://wiki.wireshark.org/SSL`
- `https://weakdh.org/`
- `https://www.openssl.org/docs/apps/ciphers.html`
- `https://goo.gl/9YUOHC`

Debugging issues

In the section, we will learn how to debug common SSL-related issues:

- Know your SSL/TLS server. It's very important how the server is configured, which TLS version is used, and which cipher suites it supports. To do this, use the nmap utility as shown:

```
root@bash :/home/ubuntu# nmap --script ssl-cert,ssl-enum-ciphers
-p 443 10.0.0.106

Starting Nmap 6.40 ( http://nmap.org ) at 2015-08-03 16:49 UTC

Nmap scan report for ip-10-0-0-106.ap-southeast-1.compute.internal
(10.0.0.106)

Host is up (0.000067s latency).

PORT     STATE SERVICE

443/tcp open   https

| ssl-cert: Subject: commonName=ip-10-0-0-106/
organizationName=Internet Widgits Pty Ltd/
stateOrProvinceName=Some-State/countryName=AU

| Issuer: commonName=ip-10-0-0-106/organizationName=Internet
Widgits Pty Ltd/stateOrProvinceName=Some-State/countryName=AU

| Public Key type: rsa

| Public Key bits: 2048

| Not valid before: 2015-07-28T14:43:45+00:00

| Not valid after:  2016-07-27T14:43:45+00:00

| MD5:    9ba5 0ea9 14b2 0793 7fe6 9329 08ce fab3

|_SHA-1: 1604 27b6 4f1c a838 9a9d db67 3136 88de effb f881

| ssl-enum-ciphers:

|   TLSv1.2:

|     ciphers:
```

```
|      TLS_ECDHE_RSA_WITH_AES_256_CBC_SHA - strong
|    compressors:
|      NULL
|_  least strength: strong
```

- The nmap output shows the server supports TLSv1.2 and one cipher suite. If the client connects with other SSL protocols or cipher suites the server doesn't support, the server will return with handshake failure. For example, connecting the same server with TLSv1.1 will return an error:

```
rootbash # curl -k --tlsv1.1 https://10.0.0.106

curl: (35) Unknown SSL protocol error in connection to
10.0.0.106:443
```

- Connecting with ciphers the server doesn't support will return a handshake error as shown:

```
root@bash # curl -k --ciphers  EXP-RC2-CBC-MD5  https://10.0.0.106

curl: (35) error:14077410:SSL routines:SSL23_GET_SERVER_
HELLO:sslv3 alert handshake failure
```

- Receiving the unknown_ca error check the following find the hash value from the certificate, private key and CSR file use the following commands:

```
bash $ openssl x509 -noout -modulus -in server.crt  | openssl md5

f637e8d51413ff7fa8d609e21cb27244

bash $ openssl rsa -noout -modulus -in  server.key | openssl md5

f637e8d51413ff7fa8d609e21cb27244

bash $ openssl req -noout -modulus -in  server.csr | openssl
f637e8d51413ff7fa8d609e21cb27244
```

The md5 hash value of csr, cer, and the private key will be the same, if csr is generated with the client private key, though the certificate is generated by using the CA (Intermediate CA) private key.

If the md5 file is the same, then verify that the certificate issued by the CA matches its path:

```
bash $ openssl verify -verbose -CAfile cacert.pem  server.crt
bash $ openssl verify -verbose -CAfile cacert.pem  client.crt
```

Useful reference for SSL testing:

- `https://www.ssllabs.com/ssltest/`
- `https://github.com/rbsec/sslscan`
- `https://testssl.sh/openssl-rfc.mappping.html`

Summary

In this chapter, we have learned how the SSL/TLS Handshake Protocol works and how to analyze it using Wireshark. We have examined sample debugging issues related to handshakes, and learned how to solve them. In the next chapter, we will continue analyzing other application layer protocols with the help of Wireshark.

5

Analyzing Application Layer Protocols

In the previous chapter, we covered the SSL/TLS application layer protocol in detail. In this chapter, we will continue with other application layer protocols (their basic flows and some generic use cases) and learn how to generate these types of traffic:

- DHCPv6
- DHCv4
- DNS
- HTTP

DHCPv6

The **Dynamic Host Configuration Protocol for IPv6 (DHCPv6)** is an application layer protocol that provides a DHCPv6 client with IPv6 an address, and other configuration information, that is carried in the DHCPv6 options.

DHCPv6 is both a Stateful Address Autoconfiguration protocol and a Stateless Address Configuration protocol.

The client and server exchange DHCPv6 message over UDP; the client uses a link-local address, DHCPv6 receives message over the link-scoped multicast address. If the DHCPv6 server is not attached to the same link, then a DHCPv6 relay agent on the client's link will relay messages between the DHCPv6 client and DHCPv6 server, as shown in the following screenshot:

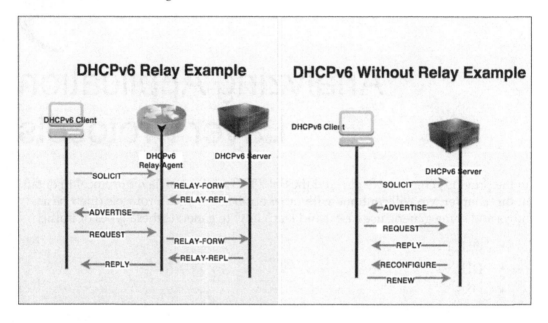

DHCPv6 Wireshark filter

Use the dhcpv6 display filter to show DHCPv6 traffic. For the capturing filter, use UDP port 547.

Multicast addresses

Multicast addresses are used by the DHCPv6 client to send datagrams to a group of DHCPv6 servers:

- For all DHCP relay agents and servers, the address is FF02::1:2 (link local)
- For all DHCPv6 servers, the address is FF05::1:3 (site local)

The UDP port information

Servers and relay agents listen for DHCPv6 messages on UDP port 547; clients listen for DHCPv6 messages on UDP port 546. To find the port information, the `netstat` command can be used:

```
[root@bash ~]# netstat -an | grep 547
udp        0      0 :::547                      :::*
```

DHCPv6 message types

DHCPv6 messages are exchanged over UDP port 546 and 547 and the messages are described in the following table:

DHCPv6 message	Description	DHCPv6 Wireshark filter	Equivalent DHCP for IPv4 message
SOLICIT	This message is sent by the client to a group of DHCPv6 servers	dhcpv6. msgtype == 1	DHCPDISCOVER
ADVERTISE	This message is sent by the server, and reveals the server availability for the DHCPv6 service, in response to the SOLICIT message	dhcpv6. msgtype == 2	DHCPOFFER
REQUEST	This message will be sent by the client and contains the IPV6 address or configuration parameter	dhcpv6. msgtype == 3	DHCPREQUEST
CONFIRM	This message will be sent by the client to confirm whether the IPv6 address is still valid for this link or not	dhcpv6. msgtype == 4	DHCPREQUEST
RENEW	This message will be sent by the client to update its lifetime or other configuration parameter	dhcpv6. msgtype == 5	DHCPREQUEST
REBIND	This message will be sent by the client if the RENEW message was not received, and it will update its IPv6 address and other configuration parameters	dhcpv6. msgtype == 6	DHCPREQUEST
REPLY	For every message sent by the client a REPLY message will be received from the server	dhcpv6. msgtype == 7	DHCPACK

DHCPv6 message	Description	DHCPv6 Wireshark filter	Equivalent DHCP for IPv4 message
RELEASE	This message will be sent by the client to release the IPv6 address and other configuration parameters	dhcpv6. msgtype == 8	DHCPRELEASE
DECLINE	This message will be sent by the client if it found that the IPv6 address is already assigned and in use	dhcpv6. msgtype == 9	DHCPDECLINE
RECONFIGURE	This message will be sent by the server to indicate that configuration parameters are updated or changed; the client will send a RENEW/REPLY or INFORMATION-REQUEST/ REPLY to get the updated configuration	dhcpv6. msgtype == 10	N/A
INFORMATION-REQUEST	This message will be sent by the client for the configuration request no IPv6 address assignment	dhcpv6. msgtype == 11	DHCPINFORM
RELAY-FORWARD	This message will be sent by a relay agent to forward a message to a server. RELAY-FORWARD contains a client message encapsulated as the DHCPv6 RELAY message option	dhcpv6. msgtype == 12	N/A
RELAY-REPLY	This message will be sent by a server to send a message to a client through a relay agent. RELAY-REPLY contains a server message encapsulated as the DHCPv6 RELAY message option	dhcpv6. msgtype == 13	N/A

Message exchanges

DHCPv6 message exchanges happen in order to obtain the IPv6 addresses, configuration (NTP server, DNS server), or RENEW/RELEASE/DECLINE of the IPv6 address, and these message exchanges are categorized in two parts:

- Client-server with a four-message exchange
- Client-server with a two-message exchange

The four-message exchange

The acronym for a four-message exchange is **SARR**, and it is used to request the assignment of one or more IPv6 addresses. The message flow is as follows:

- SOLICIT
- ADVERTISE
- REQUEST
- REPLY

Open the `DHCPv6-Flow-SOLICIT.pcap` file in Wireshark, and examine the IP assignment flow as shown:

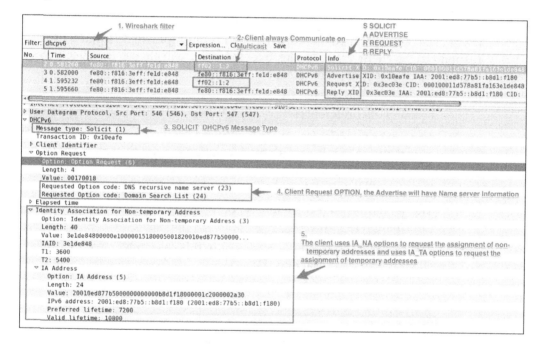

The preceding screenshot shows a SARR flow packet being captured. IPv6 is assigned to the DHCPv6 client, and the message exchanges in detail are:

- SOLICIT: The client (`fe80::f816:3eff:fe1d:e848`) sends a SOLICIT message to locate the servers. Note the destination is multicast `ff02::1:2` not the server (destination) IPv6 address:

  - The client includes its client-identifier option `dhcpv6.option.type == 1`.

- ○ The client sends it ORO option (`dhcpv6.option.type == 6`) to the server that is interested in receiving. In this case, the client has requested the name server information.

- ○ In this example, the client uses the IA_NA options to request the assignment of non-temporary addresses (`dhcpv6.option. type == 3`) and uses IA_TA options to request the assignment of temporary addresses.

- ○ The client IA address option is used to specify IPv6 addresses associated with IA_NA or IA_TA. In this example, it's associated with IA_NA.

- ● ADVERTISE: The server (`fe80::f816:3eff:fe1d:e848`) sends the ADVERTISE (`dhcpv6.msgtype == 2`) message to the client (`fe80::f816:3eff:fe1d:e848`). There can be multiple servers that will respond to the client SOLICIT message; the client will choose the DHCPv6 server based on its preference:

  - ○ The server updates the IA_NA (`dhcpv6.option.type == 3`) value based on its preferences.

  - ○ The server includes its server identifier (`dhcpv6.option.type == 2`) information. The **Server Identifier** option is used to carry DUID. The **DUID** is the **DHCP Unique Identifier**, the host identifier in IPv6. (In the case of DHCPv4, the host identifier is the MAC address.)

  - ○ The server includes the name server (`dhcpv6.option.type == 23`) information as requested in the SOLICIT message.

  - ○ The server transaction ID `0x10eafe` in this case must match with the client SOLICIT transaction ID.

- REQUEST: In this message the client chooses one of the servers and sends a REQUEST message to the server asking for confirmed assignment of addresses and other configuration information:

  ○ The client (fe80::f816:3eff:fe1d:e848) constructs the REQUEST packet and sends it to multicast ff02::1:2

  ○ The client includes a new transaction ID: 0x3ec03e.(random)

  ○ The client include server identifier information in the REQUEST packet

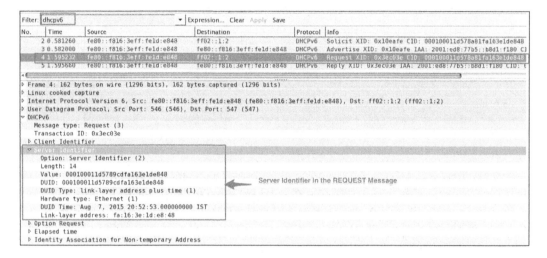

- REPLY: In the case of a valid REQUEST message, the server creates the bindings for that client according to the server's policy and configuration information, records the IAs and other information requested by the client, and sends a REPLY message by setting dhcpv6.msgtype == 7:

  ○ The server transaction ID 0x3ec03e will be the same as client DHCv6 REQUEST message transaction ID

  ○ The server will include the server identifier and the client identifier

  ○ The REPLY message will be part of a two-message exchange and a four-message exchange

The two-message exchange

The two-message exchange will be performed between client and server when IP address assignment is not required or when the DHCPv6 client wants to obtain configuration information such as a list of available DNS servers or NTP servers—for example CONFIRM-REPLY and RELEASE-REPLY. Open the sample DHCPv6-Flow-CONFIRM-RELEASE.pcap file in Wireshark, which shows that a two-message exchange was performed:

1. DHCPv6 messages CONFIRM-REPLY and RELEASE-REPLY:

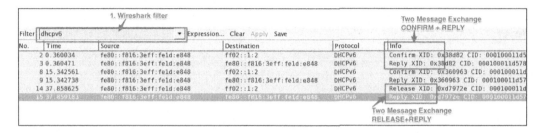

2. DHCPv6 messages INFOMRATION-REQUEST: The client sends the INFORMATION-REQUEST when the client requests configuration settings (but not addresses)—for example, DNS, NTP. As shown in the following screenshot, open the DHCPv6-Information_request.pcap file in Wireshark:

   ◦ Client will set dhcpv6.msgtype == 11:

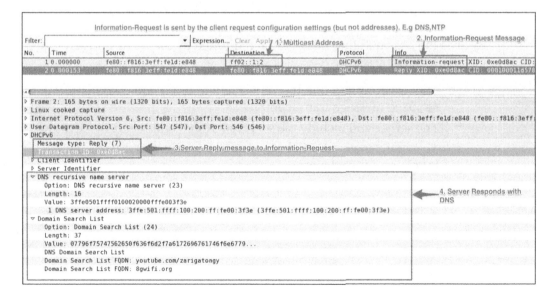

3. The rapid commit option is used to obtain the IPv6 address assignment in the two-message exchange, as shown in the following screenshot example, `DHCPv6-Rapid-Commit.pcap`. Note that rapid commit is not a separate DHCPv6 message and is part of the `SOLICIT` option:

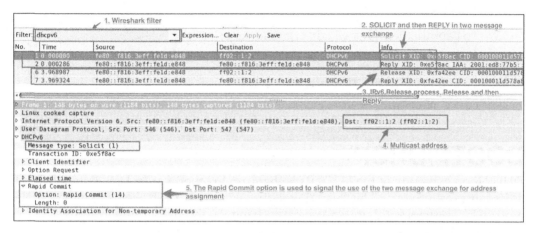

-   If a client that supports the rapid commit option intends to use the rapid commit capability, it includes a rapid commit option in the `SOLICIT` messages that it sends.

-   If the client receives a `REPLY` message with a rapid commit option, it *should* process the `REPLY` immediately (without waiting for additional `ADVERTISE` or `REPLY` messages) and use the address and configuration information contained therein.

-   If the server doesn't support the rapid commit option, then it will follow with a four-message exchange (**SOLICIT, ADVERTISE, REQUEST,** and **REPLY** known as **SARR**).

DHCPv6 traffic capture

Use `dhclient` to simulate DHCPv6 traffic over the network. For this, do the following:

1. Make sure a DHCPv6 server is set up. This example is performed over an ISC **Dynamic Host Configuration Server (dhcpd)** server.

2. Run the `tcpdump` utility to capture IPv6 traffic:

    ```
    bash$ tcpdump -i any ip6 -vv -w DHCPv6-FLOW.pcap -s0 &
    ```

    Make sure the DHCPv6 server is running in your network.

3. To capture a DHCPv6 four-message exchange (SARR):

```
bash$ dhclient -6 eth0
```

4. To capture the DHCPv6 RELEASE message:

```
bash$ dhclient -6 -r eth0
```

5. To capture the DHCPv6 CONFIRM message:

```
bash$ dhclient -6 eth0
```

6. To capture the DHCPv6 INFORMATION request:

```
bash$ dhclient -S -6 eth0
```

BOOTP/DHCP

DHCP is an extension of the BOOTP mechanism. In other words, DHCP uses BOOTP as its transport protocol. This behavior allows existing BOOTP clients to interoperate with DHCP servers without requiring any change to the clients' initialization software; the following table shows basic comparisons between these two protocols:

BOOTP/DHCP	BOOTP	DHCP (Dynamic Host Configuration Protocol)
Meaning	Bootstrap Protocol	Dynamic Host Configuration Protocol extension of BOOTP
Year	1985	1993
UDP Server Port	67	
UDP Client port	68	
Services	• IPv4 address assignment • Obtaining IPv4 configuration parameter • Limited number of client configuration parameters called vendor extensions	• IP address assignment • Leases • Support legacy BOOTP functionality • DHCP supports a larger and extensible set of client configuration parameters called options
RFC	RFC951	RFC 2131
Existence	Superseded by the Dynamic Host Configuration Protocol (DHCP)	ACTIVE; RFCs keep coming to add more features and support different technical requirements

BOOTP/DHCP Wireshark filter

Use the `bootp` filter to display BOOTP/DHCP traffic and use UDP port `67` to capture the BOOT/DHCP traffic only.

Address assignment

`DISCOVER`, `OFFER`, `REQUEST`, `ACK` protocol exchanges happen between clients and servers during network address assignment, as shown in the following screenshot. As a mnemonic, refer to this as **DORA**.

The address assignment can also be done using the Rapid Commit option for DHCPv4. Modeled on DHCPv6, it uses two-message exchanges to quickly configure the DHCPv4 client.

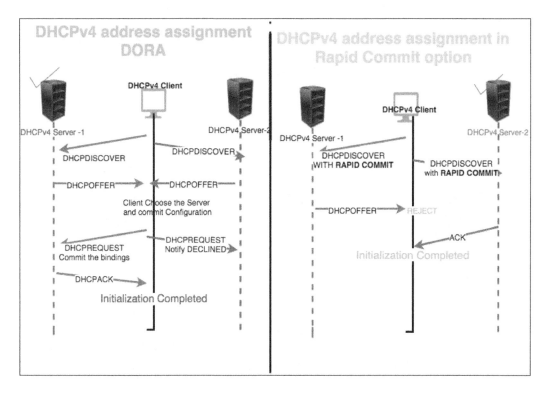

To demonstrate four-message exchange open the `DHCPv4.pcap` file in the Wireshark, as shown in the following screenshot:

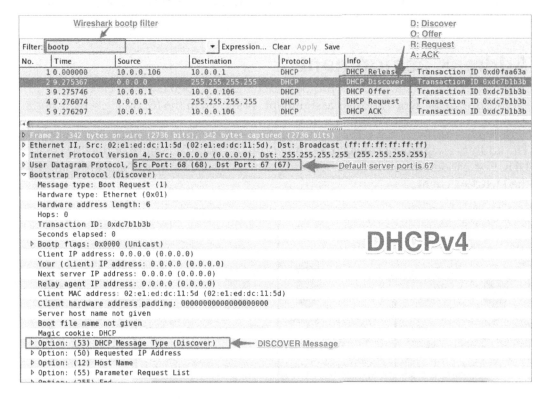

The preceding figure shows a message exchange happening between the DHCPv4 client and DHCPv4 server. This is summarized as follows:

- DISCOVER (bootp.option.dhcp == 1):
    - ○ Expand Bootstrap protocol to view BOOTP details
    - ○ The client broadcasts (255.255.255.255), a DHCPDISCOVER message, on its local physical subnet and may include the option: (55 that is bootp.option.type) parameter request list; during this time the "yiaddr" field will be (bootp.ip.your == 0.0.0.0)

- OFFER (bootp.option.dhcp == 2):
    - ○ Expand Bootstrap protocol to view BOOTP details
    - ○ The DHCP server may respond with a DHCPOFFER message that includes an available network address in the "yiaddr" (bootp. ip.your == 10.0.0.106) field

○ The DHCP server will send its option 54: DHCP server identifier and may include the other configuration parameter as requested in option 55 the `DICOVER` phase

- `DHCPREQUEST (bootp.option.dhcp == 3):`
  ○ Expand Bootstrap protocol to view BOOTP details
  ○ The client broadcasts (`255.255.255.255`) a `DHCPREQUEST` message that *must* include the option 54 DHCP server identifier to indicate which server it has selected, and may include other options specifying the desired configuration values
  ○ The DHCP server selected in the `DHCPREQUEST` message commits the binding for the client to the `db` storage and responds with an ACK

- `ACK (bootp.option.dhcp == 5):`
  ○ Expand Bootstrap protocol to view BOOTP details
  ○ The server will send the ACK to the client with the configuration parameter; during this time the IPv4 address will be "yiaddr" (`bootp.ip.your == 10.0.0.106`)
  ○ The client will verify the obtained configuration and check the IPv4 address again using the ARP protocol; if the address is in use by other dhcp clients, the client will send a `DECLINE` message to the server and restart the configuration process

Capture DHCPv4 traffic

The commands to capture DHCPv4 traffic are as follows:

- On a Windows machine:
  1. Start a Wireshark capture.
  2. Open the Command Prompt.
  3. Type `ipconfig /renew` and press *Enter*.
  4. Type `ipconfig /release` and press *Enter*.
  5. Stop the Wireshark capture.

- On a Linux machine:
  1. Start a Wireshark capture.
  2. Open the Command Prompt.
  3. Bring down the network interface:
     ```
     bash# ifdown eth0:0
     ```

4. Bring up the network interface:

   ```
   bash$ ifup eth0:0
   ```

5. Stop the Wireshark capture.

- Using dhclient:

   1. Start a Wireshark capture.
   2. Open the Command Prompt.
   3. To capture a DORA packet use:

      ```
      bash$dhclient -4 eth0
      ```

   4. Stop the capture.

DNS

DNS stands for **Domain Name System**. DNS is used by all machines to translate hostnames into IP addresses. This mechanism is used to translate names to attributes such as addresses (IPv4/IPv6) based on the query type.

DNS has three major components:

- A name space
- Servers making that name space available
- Resolvers (clients) that query the servers about the name space

This topic will focus on the resolver perspective, where the client sends a query to the server and the server answers the query. There can be multiple answers to the same query.

DNS Wireshark filter

Wireshark's dns filter is used to display only DNS traffic, and UDP port 53 is used to capture DNS traffic.

Port

The default DNS port is 53, and it uses the UDP protocol. Some DNS systems use the TCP protocol also. TCP is used when the response data size exceeds 512 bytes, or for tasks such as zone transfers.

Resource records

The following format is used by the DNS system:

Field	Description	Length	Wireshark filter
NAME	The owner name	variable	dns.qry.name == "google.com"
TYPE	Type of **Resource Record (RR)** in numeric form	2	dns.qry.type == 1 (A Record Type) dns.qry.type == 255 (ANY Record Type) dns.qry.type == 2 (NS name server) dns.qry.type == 15(MX mail exchange) dns.qry.type == 28 (AAAA quad A, Ipv6 record Type)
CLASS	Class code	2	dns.qry.class == 0x0001 (IN set to internet)
TTL	Time to live	4	
RDLENGTH	Length in octets of the RDATA field	2	
RDATA	Additional RRspecific data	Variable	

DNS traffic

In this chapter, the `dig` and `nslookup` network commands are used to query the DNS server. Open the sample `DNS-Packet.pcap` file, set the display filter to `dns.qry.type==28`, and examine the query.

In this example, client (`192.168.1.101`) is asking the name server (`8.8.4.4`) to resolve `ipv6.google.com` by setting these parameters in the query section:

- The client sets the record type AAAA record
- The client sets the hostname (`ipv6.google.com`)
- Client set the class (that is, `IN (Internet)`)
- The name server (`8.8.4.4`) responds to the client with multiple answers

- ipv6.google.com is the canonical name that equals ipv6.l.google.com

- ipv6.l.google.com has the AAAA address 2404:6800:4007:805::200e

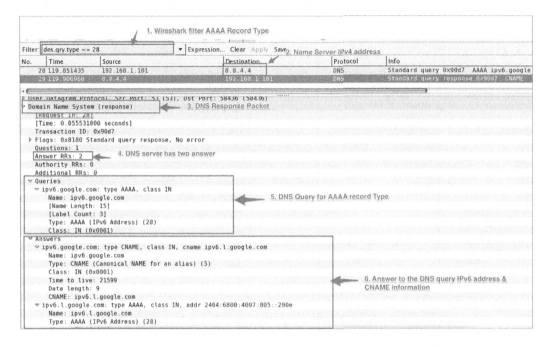

User can use the popular dig or nslookup network utility commands to query different DNS record types. Use a network capture in the background and observe the query and answer section for each command:

- Query a record type used to show the IPv4 address of the given hostname:

  ```
  bash# nslookup google.com
  ```

  ```
  bash# dig google.com
  ```

  ```
  bash# dig A +noadditional +noquestion +nocomments +nocmd +nostats
  google.com. @8.8.4.4
  ```

- Query the AXFR record type; AXFR is used to transfer zone files from the master to the secondary name server:

  ```
  bash# nslookup -type=axfr google.com 8.8.4.4
  ```

  ```
  bash# dig AXFR +noadditional +noquestion +nocomments +nocmd
  +nostats +multiline google.com. @8.8.4.4
  ```

- Query the CNAME record type. CNAME is used to set up the alias:

  ```
  bash# nslookup -type=cname google.com 8.8.4.4
  ```

  ```
  bash# dig CNAME +noadditional +noquestion +nocomments +nocmd
  +nostats google.com. @8.8.4.4
  ```

- Query the MX record type; MX is the mail exchange record:

  ```
  bash# nslookup -type=mx google.com 8.8.4.4
  bash# dig MX +noadditional +noquestion +nocomments +nocmd +nostats
  google.com. @8.8.4.4
  ```

- Query the NS record type; NS is the name server record:

  ```
  bash# nslookup -type=ns google.com 8.8.4.4
  bash# dig NS +noadditional +noquestion +nocomments +nocmd +nostats
  google.com. @8.8.4.4
  ```

- Query the PTR record type; PTR is the pointer used for reverse DNS lookups:

  ```
  bash# nslookup -type=ptr google.com 8.8.4.4
  bash# dig PTR +noadditional +noquestion +nocomments +nocmd
  +nostats google.com. @8.8.4.4
  ```

- Query the SOA record type. SOA is used to provide authoritative information such as nameserver and e-mail:

  ```
  bash# nslookup -type=soa google.com 8.8.4.4
  bash# dig SOA +noadditional +noquestion +nocomments +nocmd
  +nostats +multiline google.com. @8.8.4.4
  ```

- Query the TXT record type; this refers to the text record:

  ```
  bash# nslookup -type=txt google.com 8.8.4.4
  bash# dig TXT +noadditional +noquestion +nocomments +nocmd
  +nostats google.com. @8.8.4.4
  ```

- Query AAAA (also referred to as the quad-A record type); this will display the IPv6 address of the given hostname:

  ```
  bash# nslookup -type=aaaa google.com 8.8.4.4
  bash# nslookup -type=aaaa ipv6.google.com 8.8.4.4
  bash# dig AAAA +noadditional +noquestion +nocomments +nocmd
  +nostats ipv6.google.com. @8.8.4.4
  ```

- Query the ANY record type; this returns all record types:

  ```
  bash# nslookup -type=any google.com 8.8.4.4
  bash# dig ANY +noadditional +noquestion +nocomments +nocmd
  +nostats google.com. @8.8.4.4
  ```

HTTP

HTTP is an application layer protocol used in WWW. HTTP enables communications between the HTTP client and HTTP server. Example traffic is shown in the following screenshot. An HTTP GET request is created by the client (browser or cURL), and the HTTP server has responded with the appropriate content type:

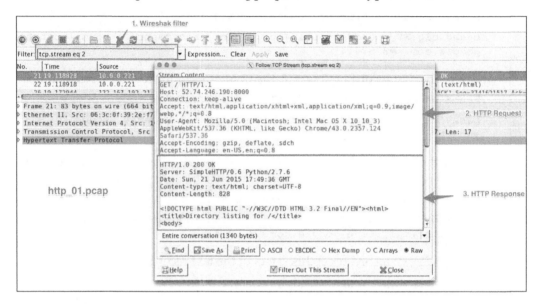

HTTP Wireshark filter

Use http to display HTTP packets only. Use TCP port 80 to filter for HTTP traffic only; port 80 is the default HTTP port.

HTTP use cases

The following example shows different use cases where Wireshark can help to analyze HTTP packets.

Finding the top HTTP response time

Open the file `http_01.pcap` in the Wireshark, and find the top HTTP response time for the request HTTP get:

1. Click on **Edit | Preferences | Protocols | TCP**, uncheck **Allow subdissector to reassemble TCP streams**. This will help in knowing how many continuation packets there are to get the actual content and it will help in fine-tuning TCP parameters—for example, setting up the TCP window size to reduce the continuation packet.

2. In the **Filter** bar, apply the `http` filter and add `http.time` as a column from the `http.response.code == 200 HTTP OK` packet.

3. Click on the **Time since request** column and make it in descending order. Find the request frame and click on the link.

Finding packets based on HTTP methods

Use Wireshark's `http.request.method` to display packets for analysis. For example, the following table describes how to apply this filter:

HTTP method	Meaning	Wireshark filter
GET	Get a specified resource example: `GET http://www.w3.org/pub/WWW/ TheProject.html HTTP/1.1`	`http.request. method=="GET"`
POST	Submits data to be processed to a specified resource	`http.request. method=="POST"`
PUT	Uploads a representation of the specified URI	`http.request. method=="PUT"`
DELETE	Deletes the specified resource/entity	`http.request. method=="DELETE"`
OPTIONS	Returns the HTTP methods that the server supports	`http.request. method=="OPTIONS"`
CONNECT	Converts the request connection to a transparent TCP/IP tunnel	`http.request. method=="CONNECT"`

Finding sensitive information in a form post

If the form contains sensitive information such as password, Wireshark can easily reveal it as HTTP is an unsecure means of transferring data over the network.

Open the `HTTP_FORM_POST.pcap` file and filter the traffic to display only the request method POST and locate the password form item, as shown in the following screenshot:

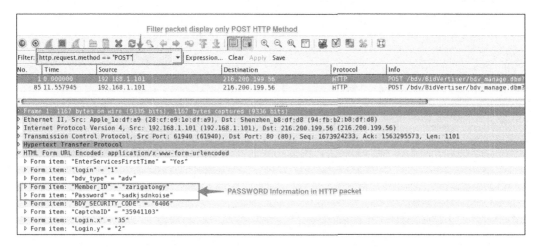

Using HTTP status code

The first line of the HTTP response contains the status code. Use the Wireshark filter `http.response.code`, to display packets based on the status code. This will be helpful when debugging the HTTP client-server interaction:

Type	Code	Meaning	HTTP Wireshark filter
Informational – 1xx	100	Continue	`http.response.code == 100`
	101	Switching protocol	`http.response.code == 101`
Successful – 2xx From: 200 To: 206	200	OK	`http.response.code == 200`
	201	Created	`http.response.code == 201`
Redirection – 3xx From: 300 To: 307	300	Multiple choices	`http.response.code == 300`
	301	Moved permanently	`http.response.code == 301`
Client Error – 4xx From: 400 To: 417	400	Bad Request	`http.response.code == 400`
	401	Unauthorized	`http.response.code == 401`
Server Error – 5xx From – 500 To-- 505	500	Internal Server Error	`http.response.code == 500`
	501	Not implemented	`http.response.code == 501`

References

The HTTP protocol:

- `https://en.wikipedia.org/wiki/Hypertext_Transfer_Protocol`
- `https://wiki.wireshark.org/Hyper_Text_Transfer_Protocol`

The DNS protocol:

- `https://en.wikipedia.org/wiki/Domain_Name_System#Protocol_transport`
- `https://www.ietf.org/rfc/rfc1035.txt`

The DHCP/BOOT protocol:

- `https://tools.ietf.org/html/rfc2131`
- `http://linux.die.net/man/8/dhclient`
- `http://www.iana.org/assignments/bootp-dhcp-parameters/bootp-dhcp-parameters.xhtml`
- `https://goo.gl/snUXkp`

The DHCPv6 protocol:

- `http://www.iana.org/assignments/dhcpv6-parameters/dhcpv6-parameters.xhtml`
- `https://tools.ietf.org/html/rfc3315`
- `https://en.wikipedia.org/wiki/DHCPv6`

Summary

In this chapter, we have learned how Wireshark helps us to analyze application layer protocols such as DHCPv6, DHCP, DNS, and HTTP. We also learned how to simulate these traffic on the wire.

In the next chapter, we will learn more about wireless sniffing.

6
WLAN Capturing

So far, we have seen packets captured on Ethernet. In this chapter we will learn how to capture WLAN network traffic, and use effective display filters for all the frames, by covering the following topics:

- WLAN (802.11) capture setup and the monitor mode
- 802.11 capturing with tcpdump
- 802.11 display filters
- Layer-2 datagram frame types and Wireshark display filters
- 802.11 auth process
- 802.1X EAPOL
- 802.11 protocol stack

WLAN capture setup

Wireshark depends on the operating system on which it's running (and on the drivers for the wireless adapter) for monitor mode support.

For Linux, the 802.11 wireless toolbar (**View | Wireless Toolbar**) provides excellent options to enable the monitor mode and set the channel for cfg80211 devices. This even supports multiple network interfaces for multi-channel captures; refer to https://wiki.wireshark.org/CaptureSetup/WLAN for detailed instructions.

The MAC OS has a wireless adapter, and the monitor mode is supported. On Windows, the monitor mode is not supported; you need a commercial adaptor for this, such as the AirPcap USB adapter.

The WLAN (IEEE 802.11) capturing process is slightly different from capturing Ethernet traffic in Wireshark. By default, when we start capturing traffic in a Wi-Fi network, it captures traffic between two endpoints (HOST-A and HOST-B). To capture the Wi-Fi traffic, Wireshark has to run in the monitor mode—**RFMON (Radio Frequency Monitor)** mode—which allows a computer with a **wireless network interface controller (WNIC)** to monitor all traffic received from the **AP (Access Point)**, as shown in the screenshot:

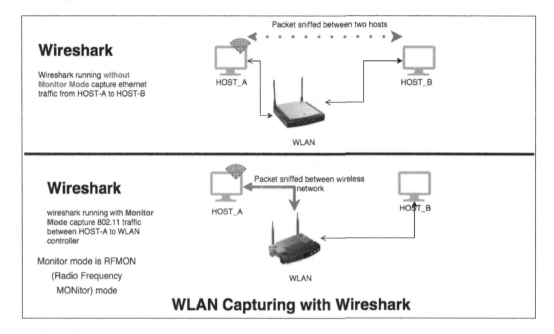

WLAN Capturing with Wireshark

The monitor mode

The monitor mode is supported only on IEEE 802.11 Wi-Fi interfaces, and only on some operating systems. To enable the monitor mode in a Wi-Fi interface, perform these steps in Wireshark:

1. Click on **Capture | Options**.
2. Select the active Wi-Fi adaptor. Double-click on the interface setting; a window will appear.
3. Enable the **Capture packets in Monitor mode** option.
4. Click on **OK**.
5. Start the capture.

You should see the following screen:

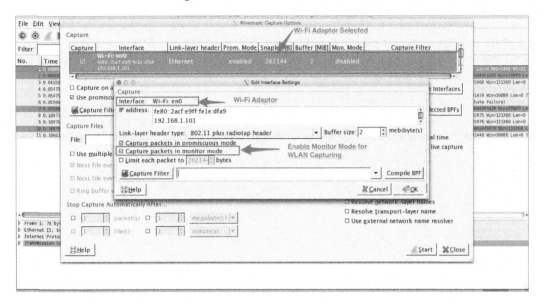

When the monitor mode is on, the adapter captures all the packets transmitted on the channel. These include:

- Unicast packets
- Broadcast packets
- Control and management packets

> Disable name resolution in the monitor mode because Wireshark will try resolving the FQDN, which results in slowness in opening the packet capture file (there is no external network in the monitor mode).

Once the packet capture starts, Wireshark will start displaying the 802.11 protocol packet exchange between source and destination, as shown in the following screenshot (or open the packet capture `802.11.pcap` file in Wireshark). Packet capture in the monitor mode will not be associated with any of the access points and the user can see only 802.11 frames, which include non-data (management and beacon) frames, as shown:

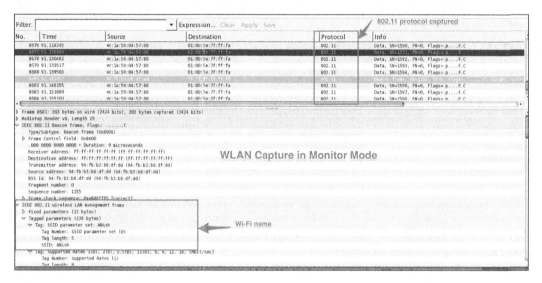

To perform a wireless packet capture using `tcpdump`, execute the following command. The `tcpdump with -I option` will turn the monitor mode on:

```
bash $ tcpdump -I -P -i en0 -w 802.11.pcap
```

The output obtained is as follows:

```
tcpdump: WARNING: en0: no IPv4 address assigned
```

```
tcpdump: listening on en0, link-type IEEE802_11_RADIO (802.11 plus radiotap header), capture size 65535 bytes
```

```
^C52 packets captured
```

```
52 packets received by filter
```

Analyzing the Wi-Fi networks

When analyzing a Wi-Fi network, it's important to go through the IEEE standard 802.11 as the source of truth as this is one of the most interesting protocols to gain a expertise on.

Wireless networks are different from a wired LAN: here the addressable unit is a station (STA), and the STA is the message destination not the fixed location when the packet is transferred to the STA.

Within the scope of the book, we are dealing with packets captured between the WNIC controller and the access point. The **access point** (**AP**) contains one station (STA) and provides access to the distribution. In this book, we will see the how Wireshark has provided display filters for analyzing Wi-Fi frames:

- `wlan`: This displays IEEE 802.11 wireless LAN frame
- `wlan_ext`: This displays IEEE 802.11 wireless LAN extension frame
- `wlan_mgt`: This displays IEEE 802.11 wireless LAN management frame
- `wlan_aggregate`: This displays IEEE 802.11 wireless LAN aggregate frame

Frames

In Layer 2, datagrams are called frames; they show all channel traffic and a count of all the frames received at the measuring STA. There are four types of frame, which are defined in the following table:

Frame type	Value	Wireshark display filter
Management	0x00	`wlan.fc.type == 0`
Control	0x01	`wlan.fc.type == 1`
Data	0x02	`wlan.fc.type == 2`
Extension	0x03	`wlan.fc.type == 3`

Let's take a detailed look at these frames one by one.

Management frames

Wireshark uses the `wlan_mgt` display filter to show all the management frames. In line with the IEEE 802.11 standard, the following management frames are defined and their corresponding values, with appropriate Wireshark display filters, are shown in the following table:

Name	Value	Wireshark display filter
association request	0x00	`wlan.fc.type_subtype == 0x00`
association response	0x01	`wlan.fc.type_subtype == 0x01`
reassociation request	0x02	`wlan.fc.type_subtype == 0x02`
reassociation response	0x03	`wlan.fc.type_subtype == 0x03`

Name	Value	Wireshark display filter
probe request	0x04	`wlan.fc.type_subtype == 0x04`
probe response	0x05	`wlan.fc.type_subtype == 0x06`
measurement pilot	0x06	`wlan.fc.type_subtype == 0x06`
beacon frame	0x08	`wlan.fc.type_subtype == 0x08`
atim	0x09	`wlan.fc.type_subtype == 0x09`
disassociation	0x0a	`wlan.fc.type_subtype == 0x0a`
authentication	0x0b	`wlan.fc.type_subtype == 0x0b`
deauthentication	0x0c	`wlan.fc.type_subtype == 0x0c`
action	0x0d	`wlan.fc.type_subtype == 0x0d`
action no ack	0x0e	`wlan.fc.type_subtype == 0x0e`

For example, by setting `wlan.fc.type_subtype == 0x08`, in the `802.11.pcap` file, the entire beacon frame will be displayed in Wireshark.

A beacon is a small broadcast data packet that shows the characteristics of the wireless network, and provide information such as data rate (max data rate), capabilities (encryption on or off), Access Point MAC address, SSID (wireless network name), RSN information, vendor specific information, Wi-Fi protected setup, and so on, where:

- SSID is the name of the AP, for example: `ANish`

- BSSID is the MAC address of the AP, for example is `94:FB:B3:B8:DF:DD`

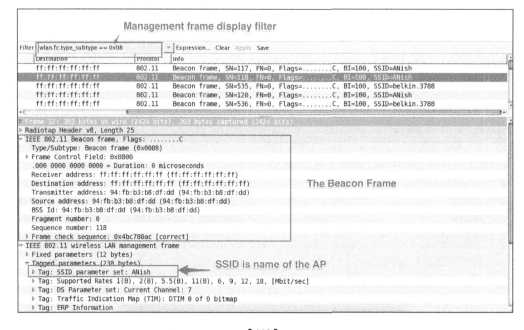

In another example, the `wlan_mgt.ssid == "ANish"` display filter will display all management frames whose SSID matches with `ANish`.

Data frames

Data frames carry the packets that can contain the payload (such as files, screenshots, and so on). Type values for data frames used in 802.11 and their corresponding Wireshark display filters are shown in the following table:

Name	Value	Wireshark display filter
data	0x20	`wlan.fc.type_subtype == 0x20`
data + cf-ack	0x21	`wlan.fc.type_subtype == 0x21`
data + cf-poll	0x22	`wlan.fc.type_subtype == 0x22`
data + cf-ack + cf-poll	0x23	`wlan.fc.type_subtype == 0x23`
null function	0x24	`wlan.fc.type_subtype == 0x24`
no data cf-ack	0x25	`wlan.fc.type_subtype == 0x25`
no data cf-poll	0x26	`wlan.fc.type_subtype == 0x26`
no data cf-ack + cf-poll	0x27	`wlan.fc.type_subtype == 0x27`
qos data	0x28	`wlan.fc.type_subtype == 0x28`
qos data + cf-ack	0x29	`wlan.fc.type_subtype == 0x29`
qos data + cf-poll	0x2a	`wlan.fc.type_subtype == 0x2a`
qos data + cf-ack + cf-poll	0x2b	`wlan.fc.type_subtype == 0x2b`
qos null	0x2c	`wlan.fc.type_subtype == 0x2c`
no data qos cf-poll	0x2e	`wlan.fc.type_subtype == 0x2e`
qos cf-ack + cf-poll	0x2f	`wlan.fc.type_subtype == 0x2f`

For example, `wlan.fc.type_subtype == 0x2A` will display all the packets that contain QoS Data + CF-Poll in the packet capture file `802.11.pcap`, as shown in the following screenshot:

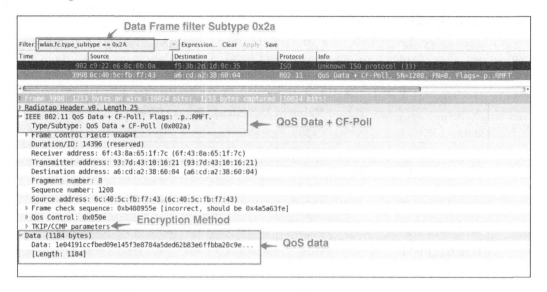

Control frames

Control frames exchange data frames between stations. Control frame ranges are 0x160 - 0x16A for control frame extensions where `type = 1` and `subtype = 6`. Values for control frames and the corresponding Wireshark display filters are shown in the following table:

Name	Value	Wireshark display filter
vht ndp announcement	0x15	`wlan.fc.type_subtype == 0x15`
poll	0x162	`wlan.fc.type_subtype == 0x162`
service period request	0x163	`wlan.fc.type_subtype == 0x163`
grant	0x164	`wlan.fc.type_subtype == 0x164`
dmg clear to send	0x165	`wlan.fc.type_subtype == 0x165`
dmg denial to send	0x166	`wlan.fc.type_subtype == 0x166`
grant acknowledgment	0x167	`wlan.fc.type_subtype == 0x167`
sector sweep	0x168	`wlan.fc.type_subtype == 0x168`
sector sweep feedback	0x169	`wlan.fc.type_subtype == 0x169`

Name	Value	Wireshark display filter
sector sweep acknowledgment	0x16a	`wlan.fc.type_subtype == 0x16a`
control wrapper	0x17	`wlan.fc.type_subtype == 0x17`
block ack request	0x18	`wlan.fc.type_subtype == 0x18`
block ack	0x19	`wlan.fc.type_subtype == 0x19`
power-save poll	0x1a	`wlan.fc.type_subtype == 0x1a`
request to send	0x1b	`wlan.fc.type_subtype == 0x1b`
clear to send	0x1c	`wlan.fc.type_subtype == 0x1c`
acknowledgement	0x1d	`wlan.fc.type_subtype == 0x1d`
contention-free period end	0x1e	`wlan.fc.type_subtype == 0x1e`
contention-free period end/ ack	0x1f	`wlan.fc.type_subtype == 0x1f`

802.11 auth process

The AP advertises its capabilities in a Beacon frame; the client (STA) broadcasts itself, using its own probe request frame, on every channel—typically (channel 11). By doing this, it determines which access points are within range.

Probe response frames contain capability information, supported data rates and so on, of the AP after it receives a probe request frame.

The STA sends an authentication frame containing its identity to the AP. With open system authentication (the default), the access point responds with an authentication frame as a response, indicating acceptance (or rejection).

Shared key authentication requires WEP (64-bit or 128-bit) keys, and the same WEP keys on the client and AP should be used. The STA requests a shared key authentication, which returns unencrypted challenge text (128 bytes of randomly generated text) from the AP. The STA encrypts the text and returns the data to AP, the AP response indicating acceptance (or rejection).

The STA sends an association request frame to the AP containing the necessary information and then that the AP will send an Association response frame that includes acceptance (or rejection). If this is accepted, the STA can utilize AP to access other networks:

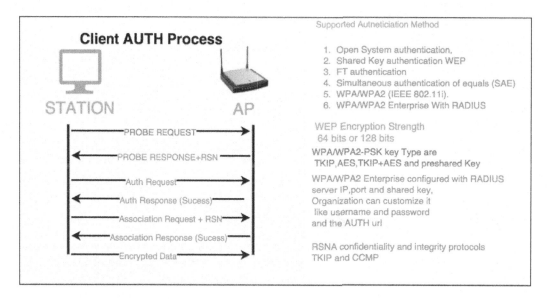

802.1X EAPOL

IEEE802.1x is based on **Extensible Authentication Protocol (EAP)**, which is an extension of **PPP (Point-to-Point Protocol)**, also known as "EAP over LAN" or EAPOL.

The IEEE 802.11 Working Group passed the 802.1x standard in 2001 to improve upon the security specified in the original 802.11 standard (IEEE, 2001).

Open the `802.11-AUTH-enabled.pcap` file in Wireshark and use the display filter `eapol` to display all the `eapol` messages only, as shown in the following screenshot. In the `eapol` packets, the session key of the device and the AP are handled.

As shown in the screenshot, all `eapol` packets are captured as 1 of 4, 2 of 4, 3 of 4, and 4 of 4.

The `eapol` packets are needed if you are trying to decrypt 802.11 traffic. The Wireshark wiki link `https://wiki.wireshark.org/HowToDecrypt802.11` is an excellent source of information on how to decrypt traffic with the help of Wireshark.

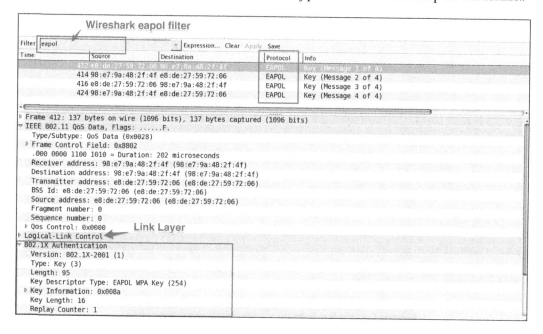

The 802.11 protocol stack

The 802.11 standard specifies a common **medium access control (MAC)** layer (the data link layer) that supports the operation of 802.11-based wireless LANs. The 802.11 MAC layer uses an 802.11 **Physical (PHY)** layer, such as 802.11a/b, to perform the tasks of carrier sensing, transmission, and receiving 802.11 frames.

Open the packet capture file `802.11-AUTH-Disabled.pcap` in Wireshark and set the display filter to `wlan.da==e8:de:27:59:72:06` to view how the data is carried using 802.11 as the transport medium.

The 802.11 QoS data frames shows that the LLC header follows IEEE 802.11; this is what is expected in the monitor mode.

The captured 802.11 looks like an Ethernet packet as the 802.11 adapter will often try to transform data packets into fake Ethernet packets and then supply them to the host.

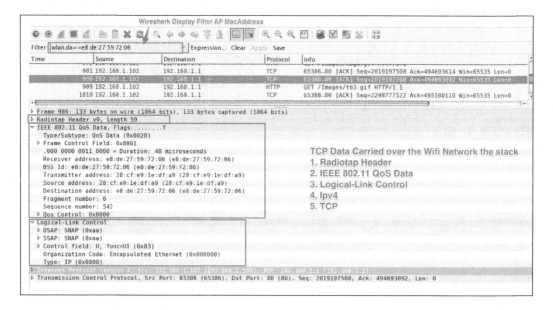

Wi-Fi sniffing products

There are other commercial (as well as open source) tools that use a form of Wi-Fi sniffing depending on the operating system and uses cases (such as WEP decryption, advance analytics, and geo location). A few of them are listed as follows:

- **Kismet** (https://www.kismetwireless.net/documentation.shtml): Kismet can sniff 802.11a/b/g/n Wi-Fi traffic.

- **Riverbed AirPcap** (http://riverbed.com): The Riverbed AirPcap adapter is used to capture and analyze 802.11a/b/g/n Wi-Fi traffic and is fully integrated with Wireshark.

- **KisMac** (http://kismac.en.softonic.com/mac?ex=SWH-1740.2) for Mac OS X: KisMac offers many of the same features as Kismet and is considered as NetStumbler for Mac. Mac users can find utility tools such as airport ID, airport utility, and Wi-Fi Diagnostics, for sniffing and diagnosing Wi-Fi networks.

- **NetStumbler** (http://www.netstumbler.com): This is used for Wi-Fi analysis.

For more information, you can visit the following links:

- `https://wiki.wireshark.org/CaptureSetup/WLAN`
- `https://en.wikipedia.org/wiki/IEEE_802.11`
- `https://wiki.wireshark.org/HowToDecrypt802.11`
- `https://www.wireshark.org/tools/wpa-psk.html`

Summary

In this chapter, we have covered Wi-Fi capture setup and discussed exactly what the monitor mode is and its pros and cons. We have also learned how the various display filters are used on the Layer 2 datagram (frames). In the next chapter, we will explore network security and its mitigation plans in greater detail.

7
Security Analysis

In the previous chapters, we learned more about protocols and their analysis techniques. In this chapter, we will learn how Wireshark helps us perform a security analysis and try to cover the security aspects in these area application and network by covering these topics:

- The Heartbleed bug
- DoS SYN flood/mitigation
- DoS ICMP flood/mitigation
- Scanning the network
- ARP duplicate IP detection (MITM)
- DrDoS introduction
- BitTorrent source identification
- Wireshark endpoints and protocol hierarchy

Heartbleed bug

The Heartbeat protocol (RFC6520) runs on top of the Record layer protocol (the Record layer protocol is defined in SSL).

The Heartbleed bug (CVE-2014-0160) exists in selected OpenSSL versions (1.0.1 to 1.0.1f) that implement the Heartbeat protocol.

This bug is a serious vulnerability that allows attackers to read larger portions of memory (including private keys and passwords) during Heartbeat response.

The Heartbleed Wireshark filter

The Heartbeat protocol runs on top of the Record layer identified as record type (24) in SSL/TLS. In Wireshark, a display filter `ssl.record.content_type == 24` can be used to show the HeartBeat message. Heartbeat messages are Heartbeat Request and HeartBeat Response.

Heartbleed Wireshark analysis

Open the `heartbleed.pcap` packet capture file in Wireshark and set the display filter to `ssl.record.content_type == 24`.

Wireshark will display only encrypted heartbeat messages. The first one is the Heartbeat Request message. In this message, the length (`ssl.record.length == 112`) of the Heartbeat Request is set to 112 bytes, as shown in the screenshot:

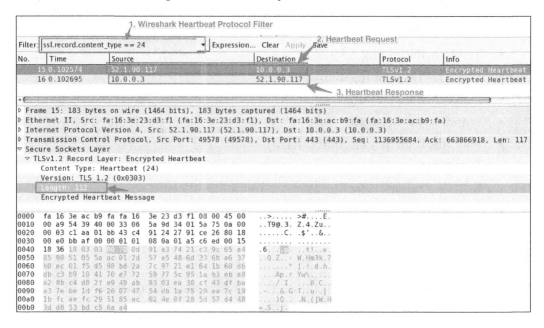

Whenever a Heartbeat Request message is send to the server, the server answers with a corresponding Heartbeat Response message.

In the given packet, the Heartbeat Response length (`ssl.record.length == 144`) is set to 144, which means the server has returned more data (32-bytes more) than expected. This extra information is known as the heartbleed; this bleed may contain sensitive information such as passwords and private keys:

```
                    Wireshark filter
 Filter: ssl.record.content_type == 24        ▼ Expression... Clear  Apply  Save
 No.    Time          Source                       Destination          Protocol     Info
        15 0.102574    52.1.90.117                  10.0.0.3             TLSv1.2      Encrypted Heartbeat
        16 0.102695    10.0.0.3                     52.1.90.117          TLSv1.2      Encrypted Heartbeat
                                        Heartbeat Response
 ▷ Frame 16: 215 bytes on wire (1720 bits), 215 bytes captured (1720 bits)
 ▷ Ethernet II, Src: fa:16:3e:ac:b9:fa (fa:16:3e:ac:b9:fa), Dst: fa:16:3e:23:d3:f1 (fa:16:3e:23:d3:f1)
 ▷ Internet Protocol Version 4, Src: 10.0.0.3 (10.0.0.3), Dst: 52.1.90.117 (52.1.90.117)
 ▷ Transmission Control Protocol, Src Port: 443 (443), Dst Port: 49578 (49578), Seq: 663866918, Ack: 1136955801, Len: 149
 ▽ Secure Sockets Layer
   ▽ TLSv1.2 Record Layer: Encrypted Heartbeat
      Content Type: Heartbeat (24)
      Version: TLS 1.2 (0x0303)
      Length: 144            Heart bleed happen, as more data is returned from the server
      Encrypted Heartbeat Message
```

The Heartbleed test

To test the heartbleed, use the following steps:

1. Install OpenSSL version (1.0.1c) from the `openssl` library:

   ```bash
   [bash ]# openssl version
   OpenSSL 1.0.1c 10 May 2012
   ```

2. Create a self-signed SSL certificate:

   ```bash
   [bash #]openssl req -sha256 -new -newkey rsa:2048 -nodes -keyout
   ./server.key -out ./server.csr -subj "/C=PU/ST=Anish/L=Test/
   O=Security Analysus /OU=Heartbleed/CN=myhost.com"
   [bash #]openssl x509 -req -days 365 -in server.csr -signkey
   server.key -out server.pems
   ```

3. Start the TLS server using the affected version of OpenSSL:

   ```bash
   [bash ]# openssl  s_server -www -cipher AES256-SHA -key ./server.
   key -cert ./server.pem -accept 443
   ```

4. Start the packet capture:

   ```bash
   [bash ]# tcpdump port 443 -s0 -w heartbleed.pcap &
   ```

If the SSL/TLS server is reachable through the public network, online filippo can be used. Other tools (such as Heartbeat Detector, which is a shell script) can also be used for this purpose:

- **Heartbleed Detector**: `https://access.redhat.com/labsinfo/heartbleed`
- **Heartbleed online test**: `https://filippo.io/Heartbleed/`

Heartbleed recommendations

The following are Heartbleed recommendations:

- Apply the patches as recommended in the OpenSSL advisory
- Change the passwords if the vulnerability is addressed.

The DOS attack

This technique is used to attack the host in such a way that the host won't be able to serve any further requests to the user. Finally, the server crashes, resulting in a server unavailable condition.

There are various attack techniques used in this topic. We will cover SYN flood and ICMP flood detection with the help of Wireshark.

SYN flood

We learned about the TCP handshake process in *Chapter 3, Analyzing the TCP Network*. In this handshake process, a connection is established with SYN, SYN-ACK, and ACK between the client and server.

In the SYN flood attack scenario, what is happening is that:

- The client is sending very fast SYN; it has received the SYN-ACK but doesn't respond with the final ACK
- Alternatively, the client is sending very fast SYN and blocking the SYN-ACK from the server, or the client is sending very fast SYN from a spoofed IP address so the SYN-ACK is sent to an unknown host that virtually doesn't exist

In all these scenarios, the TCP/IP stack file descriptors are consumed, causing the server to slow down and finally crash.

Open the SYN_FLOOD.pcap packet capture file in Wireshark and perform the following steps:

1. Click on **Statistics | IO Graph**.
2. The **IO Graph** dialog box will appear.
3. Generate four graphs for the TCP handshake message SYN, ACK, FIN, and PUSH.

The IO graph statistics show the following summary:

- The TCP connection never closes as there is no count for `tcp.flags.fin`
- The TCP connection never exchanges any data as there is no count for `tcp.flags.push`
- The count of SYN packets is very high
- The count of ACK is half of that of the SYN packets

In real scenarios, this data will be mixed up with actual packet flows, but the analysis technique will remain the same. The moment you see an unexpected growth in SYN packets or a spike in SYN packets, it's a SYN flood from DoS or from the multiple-source DDoS.

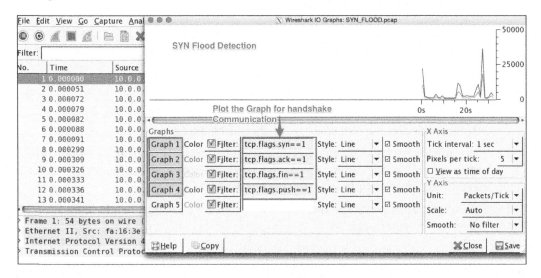

SYN flood mitigation

SYN attacks can be mitigated. The following are a few mitigation plans:

- **TCP/IP stack hardening**: The operating system decides how many times SYN, SYN-ACK, ACK will be repeated; lowering the SYN,ACK retries will help the server mitigate SYN flood attacks. A SYN cookie is used to resist SYN flood attacks. To perform all these on Linux systems, edit the `/etc/sysctl.conf` file and make changes to these entries:

```
#Prevent SYN attack, enable SYNcookies (they will kick-in when the
max_syn_backlog reached)
net.ipv4.tcp_syncookies = 1
net.ipv4.tcp_syn_retries = 2
net.ipv4.tcp_synack_retries = 2
net.ipv4.tcp_max_syn_backlog = 4096
```

```
# Increase the tcp-time-wait buckets pool size to prevent simple
DOS attacks
net.ipv4.tcp_max_tw_buckets = 1440000
```

- Restart `sycltl` to apply the changes:

  bash#sysctl -p

- IPtables firewalls can be set to deny the IPs that are causing the problem. To generate the firewall rules, use the Wireshark feature generating Firewall rules to *drop* the traffic that is causing DoS.

- For example, blocking the traffic causing the DoS:

```
# Netfilter (iptables)
iptables -A INPUT -i eth0 -d 10.0.0.3/32 -j DROP
! Cisco IOS (standard)
access-list NUMBER deny host 10.0.0.3
# IPFirewall (ipfw)
add deny ip from 10.0.0.3 to any in
# Windows Firewall (netsh)
add portopening tcp 443 Wireshark DISABLE 10.0.0.3
```

- Ports opened to the external world should be audited.

- Monitoring by creating alerts on the spikes that show unhealthy trends on the network which can result in the DoS scenario; generate the firewall rule dynamically and apply it on the targeted VM.

- Network ACLs block the traffic at the router level; introduce the IDS/IPS system to the network.

- Use the loadbalancer as the connection off-loader. In this case, if an attack happens, it will happen on the loadbalancer. The VM will remain protected. Most of the commercially available loadbalancers have the ability to defend themselves from this type of attack.

- Rate-limiting the SYN per second per IP.

- Put DoS/DDoS protection on the data center edge router (L2).

- Apply multiple levels of detection and knowing the signatures and attributes of suspected traffic locations.

- Prepare mitigation plans.

ICMP flood

Internet Control Message Protocol (ICMP) flood is also categorized as a Layer 3 DoS attack or a DDoS attack. It works as follows: an attacker is trying to flood the echo request (ping) packet with a spoofed IP address or the server is flooded with echo requests (ping packets) and not able to process the echo response for each ICMP echo request, resulting in host slowness and denial of service.

Open the `ICMP_Flood_01.pcap` packet capture file in Wireshark and perform the following steps:

1. Click on **Statistics | IO Graph**.
2. The **IO Graph** dialog box will appear.
3. Generate graphs for ICMP and ICMPv6.

As shown in the screenshot, ICMP flood has the following characteristics:

- The IO graph shows a large number of ICMP packets: nearly 80K ping requests in a short period of time
- The packet capture doesn't have the echo reply message

  This is sample data; in real environment it may vary as attackers are also learning and finding new ways to perform ICMP DoS.

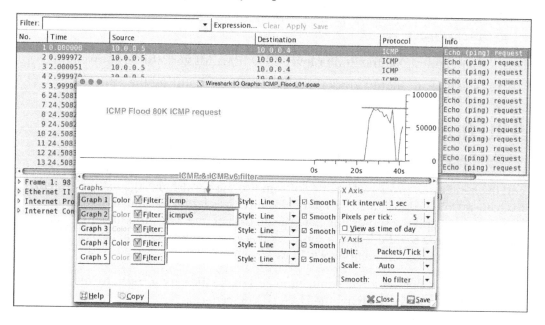

ICMP flood mitigation

The following are a few mitigation plans for the ICMP flood attack:

- **OS hardening**: On the host machine (production environment) disable the ICMP and ICMPv6 protocol through the iptables firewall:

```
bash# iptables -I INPUT -p icmp --icmp-type 8 -j DROP

bash# iptables -A OUTPUT -p icmp -o eth0 -j ACCEPT

bash# iptables -A INPUT -p icmp --icmp-type echo-reply -s 0/0 -i
eth0 -j ACCEPT

bash# iptables -A INPUT -p icmp --icmp-type destination-
unreachable -s 0/0 -i eth0 -j ACCEPT

bash# iptables -A INPUT -p icmp --icmp-type time-exceeded -s 0/0
-i eth0 -j ACCEPT

bash# iptables -A INPUT -p icmp -i eth0 -j DROP

bash# ip6tables -I INPUT -p icmpv6 –icmpv6-type 8 -j DROP

bash# ip6tables -I INPUT -p icmpv6 -i eth0 -j DROP
```

- TCP/IP stack hardening: by editing the `sysctl.conf` file and adding the following entry in this file:

```
net.ipv4.icmp_echo_ignore_all = 1
```

- Restart `sycltl` to apply the changes:

```
bash#sysctl -p
```

- Rate-limiting on the Router level if ICMP/ICMPv6 traffic is allowed

- The firewall should block the ICMP/ICPMv6 traffic on the router

SSL flood

This kind of attack happens on Layer 7 and it is difficult to detect in the sense that it resembles legitimate website traffic. In *Analyzing SSL/TLS*, we learned about SSL and the handshake process. The attacker can use the handshake against the system to create a DoS/DDoS attack. As handshake involves larger exchange of message between client and the server, for example, in case of one way auth total number of packet exchanges to established a connection is approximate 12 (that is, *3 packets TCP handshake + 9 packets SSL handshake = 12 packets exchanged*).

The attacker can flood the SSL connection and make the server busy, to just establish the connection and try to create the DoS/DDoS scenario.

Wireshark can help in identifying from which IP maximum number of packet has arrived. This feature is called Wireshark Conversations, and can be used in any kind of flood scenario (DoS attack).

Open the `ICMP_Flood_01.pcap` packet capture file in Wireshark and perform the following steps:

1. Click on **Statistics | Conversations**.
2. A conversation dialog box will appear as shown in the screenshot. An unusually higher volume of traffic is generated from source B (`10.0.0.5`) to source A (`10.0.0.4`), causing the network to slow down:

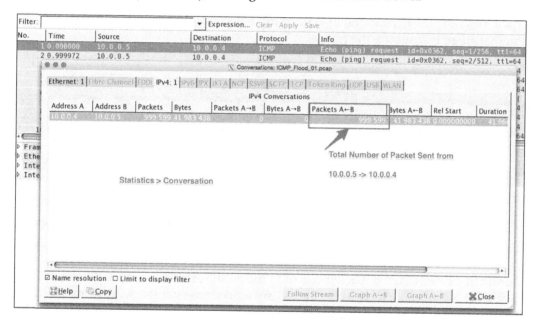

Other categories of Layer 7 attacks are HTTP/HTTPS POST flood and HTTP/HTTPS GET flood.

Scanning

In this section, we will go over the basics of vulnerability scanning and verify what is happening when the host scan is performed with the help of Wireshark.

Vulnerability scanning

Host discovery, port scanning, and OS detection are part of vulnerability scanning. During this process, vulnerabilities are identified and addressed with a proper mitigation plan by the security auditor. For example:

- The security auditor scans hosts to check that only allowed ports are open to the external world

- The hacker scans the ports to find out which services are up and running, for example during this host scan process if the DB ports are open to the outside world then the DB system is compromised for attacks.

Open the `host_scan.pcap` file in Wireshark; the sample capture shows how the external client is scanning the ports:

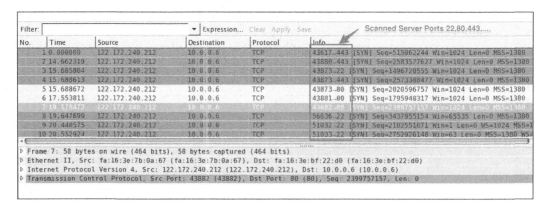

During this process, a `SYN` packet is sent to the all the ports for common services on each host, such as `DNS`, `LDAP`, `HTTP` and many more. If we get the ACK from the host, the host is considered `ACTIVE` on that port.

The security auditor or hacker can use network scanner tools to get the port, host, and OS information. For example, the `nmap` network utility command can be used to scan the active/open ports:

1. Scan standard ports in the host:

   ```
   bash# nmap -T4 -A -v 128.136.179.233
   ```

2. Scan all active ports in the host:

   ```
   bash# nmap -p 1-65535 -T4 -A -v 128.136.179.233
   ```

The online nmap tool can be found at `https://pentest-tools.com/network-vulnerability-scanning/tcp-port-scanner-online-nmap`.

SSL scans

SSL scans are done by different users (for example, security auditors and hackers) to achieve their own objectives:

- The security auditor uses a SSL scanner to find the weakest cipher suites or vulnerable SSL protocol versions present in the SSL server, to remove them
- The hacker uses a SSL scanner to hack the encrypted SSL communication by finding weak cipher suites or vulnerable protocol versions in the SSL server

An example using the nmap command to find available ciphers and the supported protocol version in a given server port 636 LDAP is as shown:

```
[root@ ~]# nmap --script ssl-cert,ssl-enum-ciphers -p 636 10.10.1.3To
find available ciphers and the supported protocol version in a given
server port 443 HTTPS
```

```
[root@ ~]# nmap --script ssl-cert,ssl-enum-ciphers -p 443 10.10.1.3
```

ARP duplicate IP detection

Wireshark detects duplicate IPs in the ARP protocol. Use the arp.duplicate-address-frame Wireshark filter to display only duplicate IP information frames.

For example, open the ARP_Duplicate_IP.pcap file and apply the arp.duplicate-address-frame filter, as shown in the screenshot:

Wireshark is providing the following information in this case:

- Usually duplicate IP addresses are resolved by the DHCP server. It has to be taken seriously when it starts showing for every IP address in this case.

- All IPs have the same Sender MAC address: `fa:16:3e:bf:22:d0` and shows as a duplicate of that IP address.

- This could be ARP poisoning—a Man in Middle attack happening in the background.

DrDoS

Distributed Reflection Denial of Service (DrDoS), also known as UDP-based amplification attacks, uses publically accessible UDP servers and bandwidth amplification factors to overwhelm a system with UDP traffic.

Open the `DrDoS.pcap` file. In this packet capture, a SYN packet is sent over a server IP address with the victim's source IP address; note the destination port is HTTP `80` and the source port is NTP port `123`, UDP. Now the server will respond with an ACK packet to the source that in this case will be the victim's IP address. If multiple servers were used, the server will flood the victim (target) with ACK packets.

There are UDP protocols (DNS, NTP, and BitTorrent) that are infected by UDP-Based amplification attacks. For more information on this, refer to alert TA14-017A published by US-CERT: `https://www.us-cert.gov/ncas/alerts/TA14-017A`.

BitTorrent

Wireshark supports the BitTorrent protocol. BitTorrent uses the Torrent file to download the content from the P2P network. The content that gets download through these programs is safe (depending on what kind of content is downloaded). Any download can contain Trojans or viruses so (this recommendation goes for any protocol used) be careful, especially when downloading any executable file or from unknown torrent URLs. All downloaded files are subjected to a scan. Open the `bittorrent.pcapng` file in Wireshark and check from that location that the content is getting downloaded.

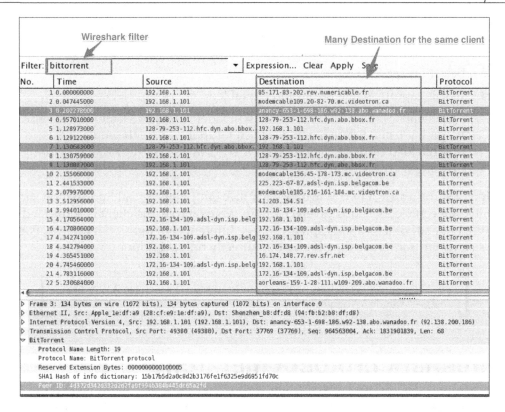

The Wireshark BitTorrent dissector is able to decode the entire download process. To check what the endpoints are from this source, do the following. Click on **Statistics | Endpoints**; an Endpoint Window will appear:

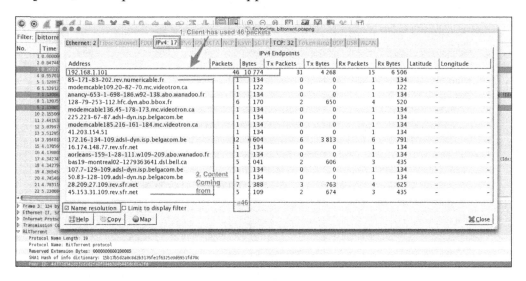

As shown in the screenshot, Wireshark has obtained the following information:

1. Filter the protocol, in this case BitTorrent.

2. Select the Ipv4 TAB.

3. In this capture, name resolution is enabled.

4. The client (`192.168.1.101`) has downloaded 10744 bytes and the content is coming from different geographical locations. Since the content was downloaded from various sources, it is always advised to scan it before opening it.

Endpoint statistics are a nice Wireshark feature. Endpoints reveal information such as outgoing connections for a given client. In this example, the client is connected to 16 different endpoint locations spread across different geographical locations. For any suspicious traffic, use the filter option directly on the Endpoint window.

 Note: Wireshark will not notify or scan for a virus; it helps to analyze the virus.

Wireshark protocol hierarchy

This feature is very useful when dealing with what protocols are running on the server. To find this, click on **Summary | Protocol Hierarchy** in the Wireshark menu. A protocol hierarchy of the captured packets will open, as shown in the screenshot:

Frame	100.00 %	166495	100.00 %	55512346	0.481	0	0	0.000
▽ Ethernet	100.00 %	166495	100.00 %	55512346	0.481	0	0	0.000
▽ Internet Protocol Version 4	99.85 %	166243	99.97 %	55493642	0.481	0	0	0.000
▽ User Datagram Protocol	51.42 %	85607	34.66 %	19243309	0.167	0	0	0.000
▽ Packet Cable Lawful Intercept	48.11 %	80108	26.90 %	14931606	0.129	0	0	0.000
▽ Internet Protocol Version 4	45.25 %	75343	25.29 %	14039605	0.122	23359	4343561	0.038
Data	28.36 %	47225	16.82 %	9335876	0.081	47225	9335876	0.081
Malformed Packet	2.80 %	4668	0.64 %	355436	0.003	4668	355436	0.003
VSS–Monitoring ethernet trailer	0.05 %	91	0.01 %	4732	0.000	91	4732	0.000
▽ Internet Protocol Version 6	2.61 %	4351	1.55 %	862607	0.007	0	0	0.000
Internet Control Message Protocol	1.76 %	2930	0.92 %	508974	0.004	2930	508974	0.004
▷ Internet Group Management Protocol	0.61 %	1016	0.52 %	286672	0.002	1004	283424	0.002
Malformed Packet	0.24 %	403	0.12 %	66005	0.001	403	66005	0.001
Internet Protocol Version 4	0.00 %	2	0.00 %	956	0.000	2	956	0.000
Malformed Packet	0.25 %	414	0.05 %	29394	0.000	414	29394	0.000
Domain Name Service	0.17 %	283	0.05 %	26178	0.000	283	26178	0.000
Network Time Protocol	0.02 %	28	0.00 %	2520	0.000	28	2520	0.000
Hypertext Transfer Protocol	0.01 %	14	0.00 %	2536	0.000	14	2536	0.000
Data	0.02 %	31	0.00 %	2666	0.000	31	2666	0.000
QUIC (Quick UDP Internet Connections)	3.09 %	5141	7.71 %	4277583	0.037	5141	4277583	0.037
NetBIOS Name Service	0.00 %	2	0.00 %	220	0.000	2	220	0.000
▽ Transmission Control Protocol	48.43 %	80630	65.30 %	36249686	0.314	33665	3799006	0.033
▽ Secure Sockets Layer	27.83 %	46335	57.99 %	32190759	0.279	46277	32187569	0.279
Unreassembled Fragmented Packet	0.03 %	58	0.01 %	3190	0.000	58	3190	0.000
Data	0.02 %	35	0.01 %	7438	0.000	35	7438	0.000
▽ Hypertext Transfer Protocol	0.12 %	194	0.36 %	200841	0.002	132	135238	0.001
Line–based text data	0.02 %	32	0.06 %	32207	0.000	32	32207	0.000
Media Type	0.00 %	6	0.02 %	8934	0.000	6	8934	0.000
Compuserve GIF	0.00 %	1	0.00 %	403	0.000	1	403	0.000
JPEG File Interchange Format	0.00 %	1	0.00 %	1494	0.000	1	1494	0.000

From the security point of view, it will give a high-level glance at all protocols that are happening over the Ethernet system. Network administrators use this information to harden the system configuration; for example, if the administrator found a DCE protocol running in the production system, after seeing this protocol hierarchy he can raise an alarm to stop this service.

Summary

Congratulation on completing this chapter and the book. So far, we have seen how Wireshark helps to analyze network protocols such as TCP/IP, DHCPv6, DHCP, and HTTP. We carried out a detailed analysis of the SSL/TLS protocol and WLAN setup capture; then we explored security-related issues and their mitigation plans. We also tried to be as practical as we can, and provided some real-time use case scenarios and their mitigation plans.

In this book, we have also emphasized other effective tools for capturing the packets, such as tcpdump and snoop. You should now be able to go forward and start analyzing other protocols not covered in this book by using it as a reference.

Index

HTTP, use cases
   HTTP status code, using 109
   packets finding, HTTP methods based 108
   sensitive information, finding in
      form post 108
   top http response time, finding 107

I

initial sequence number (ISN) 41
Interface Lists
   interface names 10
   packets, capturing with 9
Internet Control Message Protocol (ICMP)
    flood, DOS attack
   about 131
   mitigation 132
IO graph
   using 30, 31

K

key exchange, types
   Diffie-Hellman (DHE) key exchange 80
   Elliptic curve Diffie-Hellman key
      exchange 81
   RSA 81
KisMac
   URL 122
Kismet
   URL 122

M

management frames 115-117
Maximum Segment Size (MSS) 42
medium access control (MAC) layer 121
message exchanges, Dynamic Host
    Configuration Protocol for IPv6
    (DHCPv6)
   about 92
   four-message exchange 93-95
   two-message exchange 96, 97
message types, Dynamic Host Configuration
    Protocol for IPv6 (DHCPv6) 91, 92

N

NetStumbler
   URL 122
network protocol analyzer. *See* **packet**
    analyzer
No-Operation (NOP) 39, 42

O

online nmap tool
   URL 134

P

packet analyzers
   mobile packet capture 6
   tools 5
   uses 1, 2
Packet Bytes pane 27
packet capture process 4
Packet Details pane 24-27
Packet List pane 21-23
packets
   capturing 8
   capturing, with Capture Options 11, 12
   capturing, with Interface Lists 9
   capturing, with Start options 10
   file, auto-capturing periodically 13
packet sniffer. *See* **packet analyzers**
PPP (Point-to-Point Protocol) 120
protocol preference feature 29, 30

R

reset sequence
   about 49
   RST after SYN 50
   RST after SYN-ACK 49, 50
RFC675 TCP/IP
   URL 62
RFC793 TCP v4
   URL 62
RFMON (Radio Frequency Monitor)
    mode 112

Thank you for buying
Packet Analysis with Wireshark

About Packt Publishing

Packt, pronounced 'packed', published its first book, *Mastering phpMyAdmin for Effective MySQL Management*, in April 2004, and subsequently continued to specialize in publishing highly focused books on specific technologies and solutions.

Our books and publications share the experiences of your fellow IT professionals in adapting and customizing today's systems, applications, and frameworks. Our solution-based books give you the knowledge and power to customize the software and technologies you're using to get the job done. Packt books are more specific and less general than the IT books you have seen in the past. Our unique business model allows us to bring you more focused information, giving you more of what you need to know, and less of what you don't.

Packt is a modern yet unique publishing company that focuses on producing quality, cutting-edge books for communities of developers, administrators, and newbies alike. For more information, please visit our website at www.packtpub.com.

About Packt Open Source

In 2010, Packt launched two new brands, Packt Open Source and Packt Enterprise, in order to continue its focus on specialization. This book is part of the Packt Open Source brand, home to books published on software built around open source licenses, and offering information to anybody from advanced developers to budding web designers. The Open Source brand also runs Packt's Open Source Royalty Scheme, by which Packt gives a royalty to each open source project about whose software a book is sold.

Writing for Packt

We welcome all inquiries from people who are interested in authoring. Book proposals should be sent to author@packtpub.com. If your book idea is still at an early stage and you would like to discuss it first before writing a formal book proposal, then please contact us; one of our commissioning editors will get in touch with you.

We're not just looking for published authors; if you have strong technical skills but no writing experience, our experienced editors can help you develop a writing career, or simply get some additional reward for your expertise.

Wireshark Network Security

ISBN: 978-1-78439-333-5   Paperback: 138 pages

A succinct guide to securely administer your network using Wireshark

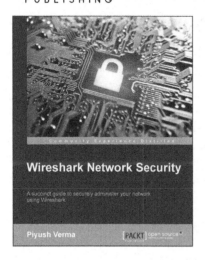

1. Make the most of Wireshark by breezing through all its features and analyzing network security threats.

2. Full of scenarios faced by security analysts along with comprehensive solutions.

3. Packed with step-by-step instructions to walk you through the capabilities of Wireshark.

Wireshark Essentials

ISBN: 978-1-78355-463-8   Paperback: 194 pages

Get up and running with Wireshark to analyze network packets and protocols effectively

1. Troubleshoot problems, identify security risks, and measure key application performance metrics with Wireshark.

2. Gain valuable insights into the network and application protocols, and the key fields in each protocol.

3. Configure Wireshark, and analyze networks and applications at the packet level with the help of practical examples and step-wise instructions.

Please check **www.PacktPub.com** for information on our titles

Network Analysis using Wireshark Cookbook

ISBN: 978-1-84951-764-5   Paperback: 452 pages

Over 80 recipes to analyze and troubleshoot network problems using Wireshark

1. Place Wireshark in the network and configure it for effective network analysis.

2. Use Wireshark's powerful statistical tools and expert system for pinpointing network problems.

3. Use Wireshark for troubleshooting network performance, applications, and security problems in the network.

Instant Wireshark Starter

ISBN: 978-1-84969-564-0   Paperback: 68 pages

A quick and easy guide to getting started with network analysis using Wireshark

1. Learn something new in an Instant! A short, fast, focused guide delivering immediate results.

2. Documents key features and tasks that can be performed using Wireshark.

3. Covers details of filters, statistical analysis, and other important tasks.

Please check **www.PacktPub.com** for information on our titles